DIALOGUE ON
THE INFINITY OF LOVE

THE
OTHER VOICE
IN
EARLY MODERN
EUROPE

A Series Edited by
Margaret L. King and
Albert Rabil, Jr.

Tullia d'Aragona

DIALOGUE ON
THE INFINITY OF LOVE

*Edited and Translated
by Rinaldina Russell and Bruce Merry*

*Introduction and Notes
by Rinaldina Russell*

THE UNIVERSITY OF CHICAGO PRESS
Chicago and London

Rinaldina Russell is professor of European Languages at Queens College, New York.
Bruce Merry is professor of Modern Languages at John Cook University
of North Queensland, Australia.

The University of Chicago Press, Chicago 60637
The University of Chicago Press, Ltd., London
© 1997 by The University of Chicago
All rights reserved. Published 1997
Printed in the United States of America
06 05 04 03 02 01 00 99 98 97   1 2 3 4 5

ISBN 0–226–13638–8 (cloth)
ISBN 0–226–13639–6 (paper)

Library of Congress Cataloging-in-Publication Data
D'Aragona, Tullia, ca. 1510–1556.
    [Diàlogo della infinità d'amore. English]
    Dialogue on the infinity of love / by Tullia d'Aragona; edited
and translated by Rinaldina Russell and Bruce Merry; introduction
and notes by Rinaldina Russell.
        p.   cm. — (The other voice in early modern Europe)
    Includes bibliographical references and index.
    ISBN 0–226–13638–8 (alk. paper). — ISBN 0–226–13639–6 (pbk.:
alk. paper)
    1. Love—Early works to 1800.   I. Russell, Rinaldina.   II. Merry,
Bruce.   III. Title.   IV. Series.
BD436.D3713   1997
128′.4—dc20   96-28841
                                                        CIP

CONTENTS

THE OTHER VOICE IN
EARLY MODERN EUROPE:
INTRODUCTION TO THE SERIES

THE OLD VOICE AND THE OTHER VOICE

In western Europe and the United States women are nearing equality in the professions, in business, and in politics. Most enjoy access to education, reproductive rights, and autonomy in financial affairs. Issues vital to women are on the public agenda: equal pay, childcare, domestic abuse, breast cancer research, and curricular revision with an eye to the inclusion of women.

These recent achievements have their origins in things women (and some male supporters) said for the first time about six hundred years ago. Theirs is the "other voice," in contradistinction to the "first voice," the voice of the educated men who created Western culture. Coincident with a general reshaping of European culture in the period 1300 to 1700 (called the Renaissance or Early Modern period), questions of female equality and opportunity were raised that still resound and are still unresolved.

The "other voice" emerged against the backdrop of a 3,000-year history of misogyny—the hatred of women—rooted in the civilizations related to Western culture: Hebrew, Greek, Roman, and Christian. Misogyny inherited from these traditions pervaded the intellectual, medical, legal, religious and social systems that developed during the European Middle Ages.

The following pages describe the misogynistic tradition inherited by early modern Europeans and the new tradition which the "other voice" called into being to challenge its assumptions. This review should serve as a framework for the understanding of the texts published in the series "The Other Voice in Early Modern Europe." Introductions specific to each text and author follow this essay in all of the volumes of the series.

THE MISOGYNIST TRADITION, 500 BCE—1500 CE

Embedded in the philosophical and medical theories of the ancient Greeks were perceptions of the female as inferior to the male in both mind and body.   *1*

Similarly, the structure of civil legislation inherited from the ancient Romans was biased against women, and the views on women developed by Christian thinkers out of the Hebrew Bible and the Christian New Testament were negative and disabling. Literary works composed in the vernacular language of ordinary people, and widely recited or read, conveyed these negative assumptions. The social networks within which most women lived—those of the family and the institutions of the Roman Catholic Church—were shaped by this misogynist tradition and sharply limited the areas in which women might act in and upon the world.

GREEK PHILOSOPHY AND FEMALE NATURE. Greek biology assumed that women were inferior to men and defined them merely as child-bearers and housekeepers. This view was authoritatively expressed in the works of the philosopher Aristotle.

Aristotle thought in dualities. He considered action superior to inaction, form (the inner design or structure of any object) superior to matter, completion to incompletion, possession to deprivation. In each of these dualities, he associated the male principle with the superior quality and the female with the inferior. "The male principle in nature," he argued, "is associated with active, formative and perfected characteristics, while the female is passive, material and deprived, desiring the male in order to become complete."[1] Men are always identified with virile qualities, such as judgment, courage and stamina; women with their opposites—irrationality, cowardice, and weakness.

Even in the womb, the masculine principle was considered superior. Man's semen, Aristotle believed, created the form of a new human creature, while the female body contributed only matter. (The existence of the ovum, and the other facts of human embryology, were not established until the seventeenth century.) Although the later Greek physician Galen believed that there was a female component in generation, contributed by "female semen," the followers of both Aristotle and Galen saw the male role in human generation as more active and more important.

In the Aristotelian view, the male principle sought always to reproduce itself. The creation of a female was always a mistake, therefore, resulting from an imperfect act of generation. Every female born was considered a "defective" or "mutilated" male (as Aristotle's terminology has variously been translated), a "monstrosity" of nature.[2]

For Greek theorists, the biology of males and females was the key to their

---

1. Aristotle, *Physics*, 1.9 192a20–24 (*The Complete Works of Aristotle*, ed. Jonathan Barnes, rev. Oxford translation, 2 vols. [Princeton, 1984], 1:328).

2. Aristotle, *Generation of Animals*, 2.3 737a27–28 (Barnes, 1:1144).

psychology. The female was softer and more docile, more apt to be despondent, querulous, and deceitful. Being incomplete, moreover, she craved sexual fulfillment in intercourse with a male. The male was intellectual, active, and in control of his passions.

These psychological polarities derived from the theory that the universe consisted of four elements (earth, fire, air, and water), expressed in human bodies as four "humors" (black bile, yellow bile, blood, and phlegm) considered respectively dry, hot, damp, and cold, and corresponding to mental states ("melancholic," "choleric," "sanguine," "phlegmatic"). In this schematization, the male, sharing the principles of earth and fire, was dry and hot; the female, sharing the principles of air and water, was cold and damp.

Female psychology was further affected by her dominant organ, the uterus (womb), *hystera* in Greek. The passions generated by the womb made women lustful, deceitful, talkative, irrational, indeed—when these affects were in excess—"hysterical."

Aristotle's biology also had social and political consequences. If the male principle was superior and the female inferior, then in the household, as in the state, men should rule and women must be subordinate. That hierarchy does not rule out the companionship of husband and wife, whose cooperation was necessary for the welfare of children and the preservation of property. Such mutuality supported male preeminence.

Aristotle's teacher, Plato, suggested a different possibility: that men and women might possess the same virtues. The setting for this proposal is the imaginary and ideal Republic that Plato sketches in a dialogue of that name. Here, for a privileged elite capable of leading wisely, all distinctions of class and wealth dissolve, as do consequently those of gender. Without households or property, as Plato constructs his ideal society, there is no need for the subordination of women. Women may, therefore, be educated to the same level as men to assume leadership responsibilities. Plato's Republic remained imaginary, however. In real societies, the subordination of women remained the norm and the prescription.

The views of women inherited from the Greek philosophical tradition became the basis for medieval thought. In the thirteenth century, the supreme scholastic philosopher Thomas Aquinas, among others, still echoed Aristotle's views of human reproduction, of male and female personalities, and of the preeminent male role in the social hierarchy.

ROMAN LAW AND THE FEMALE CONDITION. Roman law, like Greek philosophy, underlay medieval thought and shaped medieval society. The ancient belief that adult, property-owning men should administer households and make decisions affecting the community at large is the very fulcrum of Roman law.

Around 450 BCE, during Rome's republican era, the community's customary law was recorded (legendarily) on Twelve Tables erected in the city's central forum. It was later elaborated by professional jurists whose activity increased in the imperial era, when much new legislation, especially on issues affecting family and inheritance, was passed. This growing, changing body of laws was eventually codified in the *Corpus of Civil Law* under the direction of the Emperor Justinian, generations after the empire ceased to be ruled from Rome. That *Corpus*, read and commented upon by medieval scholars from the eleventh century on, inspired the legal systems of most of the cities and kingdoms of Europe.

Laws regarding dowries, divorce, and inheritance most pertain to women. Since those laws aimed to maintain and preserve property, the women concerned were those from the property-owning minority. Their subordination to male family members points to the even greater subordination of lower-class and slave women about whom the laws speak little.

In the early Republic, the *paterfamilias*, "father of the family," possessed *patria potestas*, "paternal power." The term *pater*, "father," in both these cases does not necessarily mean biological father, but householder. The father was the person who owned the household's property and, indeed, its human members. The *paterfamilias* had absolute power—including the power, rarely exercised, of life or death—over his wife, his children, and his slaves, as much as over his cattle.

Male children could be "emancipated," an act that granted legal autonomy and the right to own property. Males over the age of fourteen could be emancipated by a special grant from the father, or automatically by their father's death. But females never could be emancipated; instead, they passed from the authority of their father to a husband or, if widowed or orphaned while still unmarried, to a guardian or tutor.

Marriage under its traditional form placed the woman under her husband's authority, or *manus*. He could divorce her on grounds of adultery, drinking wine, or stealing from the household, but she could not divorce him. She could possess no property in her own right, nor bequeath any to her children upon her death. When her husband died, the household property passed not to her but to his male heirs. And when her father died, she had no claim to any family inheritance, which was directed to her brothers or more remote male relatives. The effect of these laws was to exclude women from civil society, itself based on property ownership.

In the later Republican and Imperial periods, these rules were significantly modified. Women rarely married according to the traditional form, but according to the form of "free" marriage. That practice allowed a woman to remain under her father's authority, to possess property given her by her father (most frequently the "dowry," recoverable from the husband's household in the event of his death), and to inherit from her father. She could also bequeath property to her own children and divorce her husband, just as he could divorce her.

Despite this greater freedom, women still suffered enormous disability under Roman law. Heirs could belong only to the father's side, never the mother's. Moreover, although she could bequeath her property to her children, she could not establish a line of succession in doing so. A woman was "the beginning and end of her own family," growled the jurist Ulpian. Moreover, women could play no public role. They could not hold public office, represent anyone in a legal case, or even witness a will. Women had only a private existence, and no public personality.

The dowry system, the guardian, women's limited ability to transmit wealth, and their total political disability are all features of Roman law adopted, although modified according to local customary laws, by the medieval communities of western Europe.

CHRISTIAN DOCTRINE AND WOMEN'S PLACE. The Hebrew Bible and the Christian New Testament authorized later writers to limit women to the realm of the family and to burden them with the guilt of original sin. The passages most fruitful for this purpose were the creation narratives in Genesis and sentences from the Epistles defining women's role within the Christian family and community.

Each of the first two chapters of Genesis contains a creation narrative. In the first "God created man in his own image, in the image of God he created him; male and female he created them." (NRSV, Genesis 1:27) In the second, God created Eve from Adam's rib (2:21–23). Christian theologians relied principally on Genesis 2 for their understanding of the relation between man and woman, interpreting the creation of Eve from Adam as proof of her subordination to him.

The creation story in Genesis 2 leads to that of the temptations in Genesis 3: of Eve by the wily serpent, and of Adam by Eve. As read by Christian theologians from Tertullian to Thomas Aquinas, the narrative made Eve responsible for the Fall and its consequences. She instigated the act; she deceived her husband; she suffered the greater punishment. Her disobedience made it necessary for Jesus to be incarnated and to die on the cross. From the pulpit, moralists and preachers for centuries conveyed to women the guilt that they bore for original sin.

The Epistles offered advice to early Christians on building communities of the faithful. Among the matters to be regulated was the place of women.

Paul offered views favorable to women in Galatians 3:28: "There is neither Jew nor Greek, there is neither slave nor free, there is neither male nor female; for you are all one in Christ Jesus." Paul also referred to women as his co-workers and placed them on a par with himself and his male co-workers (Phil. 4:2–3; Rom. 16:1–3; I Cor. 16:19). Elsewhere Paul limited women's possibilities: "But I want you to understand that the head of every man is Christ, the head of a woman is her husband, and the head of Christ is God" (I Cor. 11:3).

Biblical passages by later writers (though attributed to Paul) enjoined women to forego jewels, expensive clothes, and elaborate coiffures; and they forbade women to "teach or have authority over men," telling them to "learn in silence with all submissiveness" as is proper for one responsible for sin, consoling them however with the thought that they would be saved through childbearing (I Tim. 2:9–15). Other texts among the later Epistles defined women as the weaker sex and emphasized their subordination to their husbands (I Peter 3:7; Col. 3:18; Eph. 5:22–23).

These passages from the New Testament became the arsenal employed by theologians of the early church to transmit negative attitudes toward women to medieval Christian culture—above all, Tertullian ("On the Apparel of Women"), Jerome (*Against Jovinian*), and Augustine (*The Literal Meaning of Genesis*).

THE IMAGE OF WOMEN IN MEDIEVAL LITERATURE. The philosophical, legal, and religious traditions born in antiquity formed the basis of the medieval intellectual synthesis wrought by trained thinkers, mostly clerics, writing in Latin and based largely in universities. The vernacular literary tradition which developed alongside the learned tradition also spoke about female nature and women's roles. Medieval stories, poems, and epics were infused with misogyny. They portrayed most women as lustful and deceitful, while praising good housekeepers and loyal wives, or replicas of the Virgin Mary, or the female saints and martyrs.

There is an exception in the movement of "courtly love" that evolved in southern France from the twelfth century. Courtly love was the erotic love between a nobleman and noblewoman, the latter usually superior in social rank. It was always adulterous. From the conventions of courtly love derive modern western notions of romantic love. The phenomenon has had an impact disproportionate to its size, for it affected only a tiny elite and very few women. The exaltation of the female lover probably does not reflect a higher evaluation of women, or a step toward their sexual liberation. More likely it gives expression to the social and sexual tensions besetting the knightly class at a specific historical juncture.

The literary fashion of courtly love was on the wane by the thirteenth century, when the widely read *Romance of the Rose* was composed in French by two authors of significantly different dispositions. Guillaume de Lorris composed the initial 4,000 verses around 1235, and Jean de Meun added about 17,000 verses—more than four times the original—around 1265.

The fragment composed by Guillaume de Lorris stands squarely in the courtly love tradition. Here the poet, in a dream, is admitted into a walled garden where he finds a magic fountain in which a rosebush is reflected. He longs to pick one rose but the thorns around it prevent his doing so, even as he is wounded by arrows from the God of Love, whose commands he agrees to obey. The remainder of this part of the poem recounts the poet's unsuccessful efforts to pluck the rose.

The longer part of the *Romance* by Jean de Meun also describes a dream. But here allegorical characters give long didactic speeches, providing a social satire on a variety of themes, including those pertaining to women. Love is an anxious and tormented state, the poem explains, women are greedy and manipulative, marriage is miserable, beautiful women are lustful, ugly ones cease to please, and a chaste woman is as rare as a black swan.

Shortly after Jean de Meun completed *The Romance of the Rose*, Mathéolus penned his *Lamentations*, a long Latin diatribe against marriage translated into French about a century later. The *Lamentations* sum up medieval attitudes toward women, and they provoked the important response by Christine de Pizan in her *Book of the City of Ladies*.

In 1355, Giovanni Boccaccio wrote *Il Corbaccio*, another antifeminist manifesto, though ironically by an author whose other works pioneered new directions in Renaissance thought. The former husband of his lover appears to Boccaccio, condemning his unmoderated lust and detailing the defects of women. Boccaccio concedes at the end "how much men naturally surpass women in nobility"[3] and is cured of his desires.

WOMEN'S ROLES: THE FAMILY. The negative perception of women expressed in the intellectual tradition are also implicit in the actual roles that women played in European society. Assigned to subordinate positions in the household and the church, they were barred from significant participation in public life.

Medieval European households, like those in antiquity and in nonwestern civilizations, were headed by males. It was the male serf, or peasant, feudal lord, town merchant, or citizen who was polled or taxed or who succeeded to an inheritance or had any acknowledged public role, although his wife or

---

3. Giovanni Boccaccio, *The Corbaccio or The Labyrinth of Love*, trans. and ed. Anthony K. Cassell (Binghamton, NY; rev. paper ed., 1993), p. 71.

widow could stand on a temporary basis as surrogate for him. From about 1100, the position of property-holding males was enhanced further. Inheritance was confined to the male, or agnate, line—with depressing consequences for women.

A wife never fully belonged to her husband's family or a daughter to her father's family. She left her father's house young to marry whomever her parents chose. Her dowry was managed by her husband and normally passed to her children by him at her death.

A married woman's life was occupied nearly constantly with cycles of pregnancy, childbearing, and lactation. Women bore children through all the years of their fertility, and many died in childbirth before the end of that term. They also bore responsibility for raising young children up to six or seven. That responsibility was shared in the propertied classes, since it was common for a wet-nurse to take over the job of breastfeeding, and servants took over other chores.

Women trained their daughters in the household responsibilities appropriate to their status, nearly always in tasks associated with textiles: spinning, weaving, sewing, embroidering. Their sons were sent out of the house as apprentices or students, or their training was assumed by fathers in later childhood and adolescence. On the death of her husband, a woman's children became the responsibility of his family. She generally did not take "his" children with her to a new marriage or back to her father's house, except sometimes in artisan classes.

Women also worked. Rural peasants performed farm chores, merchant wives often practiced their husband's trade, the unmarried daughters of the urban poor worked as servants or prostitutes. All wives produced or embellished textiles and did the housekeeping, while wealthy ones managed servants. These labors were unpaid or poorly paid, but often contributed substantially to family wealth.

WOMEN'S ROLES: THE CHURCH. Membership in a household, whether a father's or a husband's, meant for women a lifelong subordination to others. In western Europe, the Roman Catholic Church offered an alternative to the career of wife and mother. A woman could enter a convent parallel in function to the monasteries for men that evolved in the early Christian centuries.

In the convent, a woman pledged herself to a celibate life, lived according to strict community rules, and worshipped daily. Often the convent offered training in Latin, allowing some women to become considerable scholars and authors, as well as scribes, artists, and musicians. For women who chose the conventual life, the benefits could be enormous, but for numerous others placed in convents by paternal choice, the life could be restrictive and burdensome.

The conventual life declined as an alternative for women as the modern age approached. Reformed monastic institutions resisted responsibility for related female orders. The church increasingly restricted female institutional life by insisting on closer male supervision.

Women often sought other options. Some joined the communities of laywomen that sprang up spontaneously in the thirteenth century in the urban zones of western Europe, especially in Flanders and Italy. Some joined the heretical movements that flourished in late medieval Christendom, whose anticlerical and often antifamily positions particularly appealed to women. In these communities, some women were acclaimed as "holy women" or "saints," while others often were condemned as frauds or heretics.

In all, though the options offered to women by the church were sometimes less than satisfactory, sometimes they were richly rewarding. After 1520, the convent remained an option only in Roman Catholic territories. Protestantism engendered an ideal of marriage as a heroic endeavor and appeared to place husband and wife on a more equal footing. Sermons and treatises, however, still called for female subordination and obedience.

THE OTHER VOICE, 1300–1700

Misogyny was so long-established in European culture when the modern era opened that to dismantle it was a monumental labor. The process began as part of a larger cultural movement that entailed the critical reexamination of ideas inherited from the ancient and medieval past. The humanists launched that critical reexamination.

THE HUMANIST FOUNDATION. Originating in Italy in the fourteenth century, humanism quickly became the dominant intellectual movement in Europe. Spreading in the sixteenth century from Italy to the rest of Europe, it fueled the literary, scientific, and philosophical movements of the era and laid the basis for the eighteenth-century Enlightenment.

Humanists regarded the scholastic philosophy of medieval universities as out of touch with the realities of urban life. They found in the rhetorical discourse of classical Rome a language adapted to civic life and public speech. They learned to read, speak, and write classical Latin, and eventually classical Greek. They founded schools to teach others to do so, establishing the pattern for elementary and secondary education for the next three hundred years.

In the service of complex government bureaucracies, humanists employed their skills to write eloquent letters, deliver public orations, and formulate public policy. They developed new scripts for copying manuscripts and used the new printing press for the dissemination of texts, for which they created methods of critical editing.

Humanism was a movement led by males who accepted the evaluation of women in ancient texts and generally shared the misogynist perceptions of their culture. (Female humanists, as will be seen, did not.) Yet humanism also opened the door to the critique of the misogynist tradition. By calling authors, texts, and ideas into question, it made possible the fundamental rereading of the whole intellectual tradition that was required in order to free women from cultural prejudice and social subordination.

A DIFFERENT CITY. The other voice first appeared when, after so many centuries, the accumulation of misogynist concepts evoked a response from a capable woman female defender: Christine de Pizan. Introducing her *Book of the City of Ladies* (1405), she described how she was affected by reading Mathéolus's *Lamentations*: "Just the sight of this book . . . made me wonder how it happened that so many different men . . . are so inclined to express both in speaking and in their treatises and writings so many wicked insults about women and their behavior."[4] These statements impelled her to detest herself "and the entire feminine sex, as though we were monstrosities in nature."[5]

The remainder of the *Book of the City of Ladies* presents a justification of the female sex and a vision of an ideal community of women. A pioneer, she has not only received the misogynist message, but she rejects it. From the fourteenth to seventeenth century, a huge body of literature accumulated that responded to the dominant tradition.

The result was a literary explosion consisting of works by both men and women, in Latin and in vernacular languages: works enumerating the achievements of notable women; works rebutting the main accusations made against women; works arguing for the equal education of men and women; works defining and redefining women's proper role in the family, at court, and in public; and describing women's lives and experiences. Recent monographs and articles have begun to hint at the great range of this phenomenon, involving probably several thousand titles. The protofeminism of these "other voices" constitute a significant fraction of the literary product of the early modern era.

THE CATALOGUES. Around 1365, the same Boccaccio whose *Corbaccio* rehearses the usual charges against female nature, wrote another work, *Concerning Famous Women*. A humanist treatise drawing on classical texts, it praised 106 notable women—one hundred of them from pagan Greek and Roman antiquity, and six from the religious and cultural tradition since antiquity—and helped make all readers aware of a sex normally condemned or forgotten. Boc-

4. Christine de Pizan, *The Book of the City of Ladies*, trans. Earl Jeffrey Richards; Foreword Marina Warner (New York, 1982), I.1.1., pp. 3–4.
5. Ibid., I.1.1–2, p. 5.

caccio's outlook, nevertheless, was misogynist, for it singled out for praise those women who possessed the traditional virtues of chastity, silence, and obedience. Women who were active in the public realm, for example, rulers and warriors, were depicted as suffering terrible punishments for entering into the masculine sphere. Women were his subject, but Boccaccio's standard remained male.

Christine de Pizan's *Book of the City of Ladies* contains a second catalogue, one responding specifically to Boccaccio's. Where Boccaccio portrays female virtue as exceptional, she depicts it as universal. Many women in history were leaders, or remained chaste despite the lascivious approaches of men, or were visionaries and brave martyrs.

The work of Boccaccio inspired a series of catalogues of illustrious women of the biblical, classical, Christian, and local past: works by Alvaro de Luna, Jacopo Filippo Foresti (1497), Brantôme, Pierre Le Moyne, Pietro Paolo de Ribera (who listed 845 figures), and many others. Whatever their embedded prejudices, these catalogues of illustrious women drove home to the public the possibility of female excellence.

THE DEBATE. At the same time, many questions remained: Could a woman be virtuous? Could she perform noteworthy deeds? Was she even, strictly speaking, of the same human species as men? These questions were debated over four centuries, in French, German, Italian, Spanish and English, by authors male and female, among Catholics, Protestants and Jews, in ponderous volumes and breezy pamphlets. The whole literary phenomenon has been called the *querelle des femmes*, the "Woman Question."

The opening volley of this battle occurred in the first years of the fifteenth century, in a literary debate sparked by Christine de Pizan. She exchanged letters critical of Jean de Meun's contribution to the *Romance of the Rose* with two French humanists and royal secretaries, Jean de Montreuil and Gontier Col. When the matter became public, Jean Gerson, one of Europe's leading theologians, supported de Pizan's arguments against de Meun, for the moment silencing the opposition.

The debate resurfaced repeatedly over the next two hundred years. *The Triumph of Women* (1438) by Juan Rodríguez de la Camara (or Juan Rodríguez del Padron) struck a new note by presenting arguments for the superiority of women to men. *The Champion of Women* (1440–42) by Martin Le Franc addresses once again the misogynist claims of *The Romance of the Rose* and offers counterevidence of female virtue and achievement.

A cameo of the debate on women is included in the *Courtier*, one of the most-read books of the era, published by the Italian Baldassare Castiglione in 1528 and immediately translated into other European vernaculars. The

Courtier depicts a series of evenings at the court of the Duke of Urbino in which many men and some women of the highest social stratum amuse themselves by discussing a range of literary and social issues. The "woman question" is a pervasive theme throughout, and the third of its four books is devoted entirely to that issue.

In a verbal duel, Gasparo Pallavicino and Giuliano de' Medici present the main claims of the two traditions—the prevailing misogynist one, and the newly emerging alternative one. Gasparo argues the innate inferiority of women and their inclination to vice. Only in bearing children do they profit the world. Giuliano counters that women share the same spiritual and mental capacities as men and may excel in wisdom and action. Men and women are of the same essence: just as no stone can be more perfectly a stone than another, so no human being can be more perfectly human than others, whether male or female. It was an astonishing assertion, boldly made to an audience as large as all Europe.

THE TREATISES. Humanism provided the materials for a positive counter-concept to the misogyny embedded in scholastic philosophy and law and inherited from the Greek, Roman, and Christian pasts. A series of humanist treatises on marriage and family, education and deportment, and on the nature of women helped construct these new perspectives.

The works by Francesco Barbaro and Leon Battista Alberti, respectively *On Marriage* (1415) and *On the Family* (1434–37), far from defending female equality, reasserted women's responsibilities for rearing children and managing the housekeeping while being obedient, chaste, and silent. Nevertheless, they served the cause of reexamining the issue of women's nature by placing domestic issues at the center of scholarly concern and reopening the pertinent classical texts. In addition, Barbaro emphasized the companionate nature of marriage and the importance of a wife's spiritual and mental qualities for the well-being of the family.

These themes reappear in later humanist works on marriage and the education of women by Juan Luis Vives and Erasmus. Both were moderately sympathetic to the condition of women, without reaching beyond the usual masculine prescriptions for female behavior.

An outlook more favorable to women characterizes the nearly unknown work *In Praise of Women* (ca. 1487) by the Italian humanist Bartolomeo Goggio. In addition to providing a catalogue of illustrious women, Gogio argued that male and female are the same in essence, but that women (reworking from quite a new angle the Adam and Eve narrative) are actually superior. In the same vein, the Italian humanist Mario Equicola asserted the spiritual equality of men and women in *On Women* (1501). In 1525, Galeazzo Flavio Capra (or

Capella) published his work *On the Excellence and Dignity of Women*. This humanist tradition of treatises defending the worthiness of women culminates in the work of Henricus Cornelius Agrippa *On the Nobility and Preeminence of the Female Sex*. No work by a male humanist more succinctly or explicitly presents the case for female dignity.

THE WITCH BOOKS. While humanists grappled with the issues pertaining to women and family, other learned men turned their attention to what they perceived as a very great problem: witches. Witch-hunting manuals, explorations of the witch phenomenon, and even defenses of witches are not at first glance pertinent to the tradition of the other voice. But they do relate in this way: most accused witches were women. The hostility aroused by supposed witch activity is comparable to the hostility aroused by women. The evil deeds the victims of the hunt were charged with were exaggerations of the vices to which, many believed, all women were prone.

The connection between the witch accusation and the hatred of women is explicit in the notorious witch-hunting manual, *The Hammer of Witches* (1486), by two Dominican inquisitors, Heinrich Krämer and Jacob Sprenger. Here the inconstancy, deceitfulness, and lustfulness traditionally associated with women are depicted in exaggerated form as the core features of witch behavior. These inclined women to make a bargain with the devil—sealed by sexual intercourse—by which they acquired unholy powers. Such bizarre claims, far from being rejected by rational men, were broadcast by intellectuals. The German Ulrich Molitur, the Frenchman Nicolas Rémy, the Italian Stefano Guazzo coolly informed the public of sinister orgies and midnight pacts with the devil. The celebrated French jurist, historian, and political philosopher Jean Bodin argued that, because women were especially prone to diabolism, regular legal procedures could properly be suspended in order to try those accused of this "exceptional crime."

A few experts, such as the physician Johann Weyer, a student of Agrippa's, raised their voices in protest. In 1563, Weyer explained the witch phenomenon thus, without discarding belief in diabolism: the devil deluded foolish old women afflicted by melancholia, causing them to believe that they had magical powers. His rational skepticism, which had good credibility in the community of the learned, worked to revise the conventional views of women and witchcraft.

WOMEN'S WORKS. To the many categories of works produced on the question of women's worth must be added nearly all works written by women. A woman writing was in herself a statement of women's claim to dignity.

Only a few women wrote anything prior to the dawn of the modern era, for three reasons. First, they rarely received the education that would enable them to write. Second, they were not admitted to the public roles—as administrator, bureaucrat, lawyer or notary, university professor—in which they might gain knowledge of the kinds of things the literate public thought worth writing about. Third, the culture imposed silence upon women, considering speaking out a form of unchastity. Given these conditions, it is remarkable that any women wrote. Those who did before the fourteenth century were almost always nuns or religious women whose isolation made their pronouncements more acceptable.

From the fourteenth century on, the volume of women's writings crescendoed. Women continued to write devotional literature, although not always as cloistered nuns. They also wrote diaries, often intended as keepsakes for their children; books of advice to their sons and daughters; letters to family members and friends; and family memoirs, in a few cases elaborate enough to be considered histories.

A few women wrote works directly concerning the "woman question," and some of these, such as the humanists Isotta Nogarola, Cassandra Fedele, Laura Cereta, and Olimpia Morata, were highly trained. A few were professional writers, living by the income of their pen: the very first among them Christine de Pizan, noteworthy in this context as in so many others. In addition to *The Book of the City of Ladies* and her critiques of *The Romance of the Rose*, she wrote *The Treasure of the City of Ladies* (a guide to social decorum for women), an advice book for her son, much courtly verse, and a full-scale history of the reign of king Charles V of France.

WOMEN PATRONS. Women who did not themselves write but encouraged others to do so boosted the development of an alternative tradition. Highly placed women patrons supported authors, artists, musicians, poets, and learned men. Such patrons, drawn mostly from the Italian elites and the courts of northern Europe, figure disproportionately as the dedicatees of the important works of early feminism.

For a start, it might be noted that the catalogues of Boccaccio and Alvaro de Luna were dedicated to the Florentine noblewoman Andrea Acciaiuoli and to Doña María, first wife of King Juan II of Castile, while the French translation of Boccaccio's work was commissioned by Anne of Brittany, wife of King Charles VIII of France. The humanist treatises of Goggio, Equicola, Vives, and Agrippa were dedicated, respectively, to Eleanora of Aragon, wife of Ercole I d'Este, duke of Ferrara; to Margherita Cantelma of Mantua; to Catherine of Aragon, wife of King Henry VIII of England; and to Margaret, duchess of Austria and regent of the Netherlands. As late as 1696, Mary Astell's *Serious Proposal to the Ladies, for the Advancement of Their True and Greatest Interest* was dedicated to Princess Ann of Denmark.

These authors presumed that their efforts would be welcome to female patrons, or they may have written at the bidding of those patrons. Silent themselves, perhaps even unresponsive, these loftily placed women helped shape the tradition of the other voice.

THE ISSUES. The literary forms and patterns in which the tradition of the other voice presented itself have now been sketched. It remains to highlight the major issues about which this tradition crystallizes. In brief, there are four problems to which our authors return again and again, in plays and catalogues, in verse and in letters, in treatises and dialogues, in every language: the problem of chastity; the problem of power; the problem of speech; and the problem of knowledge. Of these the greatest, preconditioning the others, is the problem of chastity.

THE PROBLEM OF CHASTITY. In traditional European culture, as in those of antiquity and others around the globe, chastity was perceived as woman's quintessential virtue—in contrast to courage, or generosity, or leadership, or rationality, seen as virtues characteristic of men. Opponents of women charged them with insatiable lust. Women themselves and their defenders—without disputing the validity of the standard—responded that women were capable of chastity.

The requirement of chastity kept women at home, silenced them, isolated them, left them in ignorance. It was the source of all other impediments. Why was it so important to the society of men, of whom chastity was not required, and who, more often than not, considered it their right to violate the chastity of any woman they encountered?

Female chastity ensured the continuity of the male-headed household. If a man's wife was not chaste, he could not be sure of the legitimacy of his offspring. If they were not his, and they acquired his property, it was not his household, but some other man's, that had endured. If his daughter was not chaste, she could not be transferred to another man's household as his wife, and he was dishonored.

The whole system of the integrity of the household and the transmission of property was bound up in female chastity. Such a requirement only pertained to property-owning classes, of course. Poor women could not expect to maintain their chastity, least of all if they were in contact with high-status men to whom all women but those of their own household were prey.

In Catholic Europe, the requirement of chastity was further buttressed by moral and religious imperatives. Original sin was inextricably linked with the sexual act. Virginity was seen as heroic virtue, far more impressive than, say, the avoidance of idleness or greed. Monasticism, the cultural institution that dominated medieval Europe for centuries, was grounded in the renunciation of the flesh. The Catholic reform of the eleventh century imposed a similar standard on all the clergy and a heightened awareness of sexual requirements on all the laity. Although men were asked to be chaste, female unchastity was much worse: it led to the devil, as Eve had led mankind to sin.

To such requirements, women and their defenders protested their innocence. More, following the example of holy women who had escaped the requirements of family and sought the religious life, some women began to conceive of female communities as alternatives both to family and to the cloister. Christine de Pizan's city of ladies was such a community. Moderata Fonte and Mary Astell envisioned others. The luxurious salons of the French *précieuses* of the seventeenth century, or the comfortable English drawing rooms of the next, may have been born of the same impulse. Here women might not only escape, if briefly, the subordinate position that life in the family entailed, but they might make claims to power, exercise their capacity for speech, and display their knowledge.

THE PROBLEM OF POWER. Women were excluded from power: the whole cultural tradition insisted upon it. Only men were citizens, only men bore arms, only men could be chiefs or lords or kings. There were exceptions which did not disprove the rule, when wives or widows or mothers took the place of men, awaiting their return or the maturation of a male heir. A woman who attempted to rule in her own right was perceived as an anomaly, a monster, at once a deformed woman and an insufficient male, sexually confused and, consequently, unsafe.

The association of such images with women who held or sought power explains some otherwise odd features of early modern culture. Queen Elizabeth I of England, one of the few women to hold full regal authority in European history, played with such male/female images—positive ones, of course—in representing herself to her subjects. She was a prince, and manly, even though she was female. She was also (she claimed) virginal, a condition absolutely essential if she was to avoid the attacks of her opponents. Catherine de' Medici, who ruled France as widow and regent for her sons, also adopted such imagery in defining her position. She chose as one symbol the figure of Artemisia, an androgynous ancient warrior-heroine, who combined a female persona with masculine powers.

Power in a woman, without such sexual imagery, seems to have been indigestible by the culture. A rare note was struck by the Englishman Sir Thomas Elyot in his *Defence of Good Women* (1540), justifying both women's participation in civic life and prowess in arms. The old tune was sung by the Scots reformer John Knox in his *First Blast of the Trumpet against the Monstrous Regiment of Women* (1558), for whom rule by women, defective in nature, was a hideous contradiction in terms.

The confused sexuality of the imagery of female potency was not reserved for rulers. Any woman who excelled was likely to be called an Amazon, recalling the self-mutilated warrior women of antiquity who repudiated all men, gave up their sons, and raised only their daughters. She was often said to have "exceeded her sex," or to have possessed "masculine virtue"—as the very fact of conspicuous excellence conferred masculinity, even on the female subject. The catalogues of notable women often showed those female heroes dressed in armor, armed to the teeth, like men. Amazonian heroines romp through the epics of the age—Ariosto's *Orlando Furioso* (1532), Spenser's *Faerie Queene* (1590–1609). Excellence in a woman was perceived as a claim for power, and power was reserved for the masculine realm. A woman who possessed either was masculinized and lost title to her own female identity.

THE PROBLEM OF SPEECH. Just as power had a sexual dimension when it was claimed by women, so did speech. A good woman spoke little. Excessive speech was an indication of unchastity. By speech, women seduced men. Eve had lured Adam into sin by her speech. Accused witches were commonly accused of having spoken abusively, or irrationally, or simply too much. As enlightened a figure as Francesco Barbaro insisted on silence in a woman, which he linked to her perfect unanimity with her husband's will and her unblemished virtue (her chastity). Another Italian humanist, Leonardo Bruni, in advising a noblewoman on her studies, barred her not from speech, but from public speaking. That was reserved for men.

Related to the problem of speech was that of costume, another, if silent, form of self-expression. Assigned the task of pleasing men as their primary occupation, elite women often tended to elaborate costume, hairdressing, and the use of cosmetics. Clergy and secular moralists alike condemned these practices. The appropriate function of costume and adornment was to announce the status of a woman's husband or father. Any further indulgence in adornment was akin to unchastity.

THE PROBLEM OF KNOWLEDGE. When the Italian noblewoman Isotta Nogarola had begun to attain a reputation as a humanist, she was accused of incest—a telling instance of the association of learning in women with unchastity. That chilling association inclined any woman who was educated to deny that she was, or to make exaggerated claims of heroic chastity.

If educated women were pursued with suspicions of sexual misconduct, women seeking an education faced an even more daunting obstacle: the assumption that women were by nature incapable of learning, that reason was a particularly masculine ability. Just as they proclaimed their chastity, women and their defenders insisted upon their capacity for learning. The major work by a male writer on female education—*On the Education of a Christian Woman*, by Juan Luis Vives (1523)—granted female capacity for intellection, but argued still that a woman's whole education was to be shaped around the requirement of chastity and a future within the household. Female writers of the following generations—Marie de Gournay in France, Anna Maria van Schurman in Holland, Mary Astell in England—began to envision other possibilities.

The pioneers of female education were the Italian women humanists who managed to attain a Latin literacy and knowledge of classical and Christian literature equivalent to that of prominent men. Their works implicitly and explicitly raise questions about women's social roles, defining problems that beset women attempting to break out of the cultural limits that had bound them. Like Christine de Pizan, who achieved an advanced education through her father's tutoring and her own devices, their bold questioning makes clear the importance of training. Only when women were educated to the same standard as male leaders would they be able to raise that other voice and insist on their dignity as human beings morally, intellectually, and legally equal to men.

THE OTHER VOICE. The other voice, a voice of protest, was mostly female, but also male. It spoke in the vernaculars and in Latin, in treatises and dialogues, plays and poetry, letters and diaries and pamphlets. It battered at the wall of misogynist beliefs that encircled women and raised a banner announcing its claims. The female was equal (or even superior) to the male in essential nature—moral, spiritual, intellectual. Women were capable of higher education, of holding positions of power and influence in the public realm, and of speaking and writing persuasively. The last bastion of masculine supremacy, centered on the notions of a woman's primary domestic responsibility and the requirement of female chastity, was not as yet assaulted—although visions of productive female communities as alternatives to the family indicated an awareness of the problem.

During the period 1300 to 1700, the other voice remained only a voice, and one only dimly heard. It did not result—yet—in an alteration of social patterns. Indeed, to this day, they have not entirely been altered. Yet the call for justice issued as long as six centuries ago by those writing in the tradition of the other voice must be recognized as the source and origin of the mature feminist tradition and of the realignment of social institutions accomplished in the modern age.

We would like to thank the volume editors in this series, who responded with many suggestions to an earlier draft of this introduction, making it a collaborative enterprise. Many of their suggestions and criticisms have resulted in revisions of this introduction, though we remain responsible for the final product.

Margaret L. King
Albert Rabil, Jr.

PROJECTED TITLES IN THE SERIES

Henricus Cornelius Agrippa, *Declamation on the Nobility and Preeminence of the Female Sex*, translated and edited by Albert Rabil, Jr.

Tullia d'Aragona, *Dialogue on the Infinity of Love*, edited and translated by Rinaldina Russell and Bruce Merry

Laura Cereta, *Collected Letters of a Renaissance Feminist*, edited and translated by Diana Robin

Cassandra Fedele, *Letters and Orations*, edited and translated by Diana Robin

Cecilia Ferrazzi, *Autobiography of an Aspiring Saint*, transcribed, translated, and annotated by Anne Jacobson Schutte

Moderata Fonte, *The Worth of Women*, edited and translated by Virginia Cox

Veronica Franco, *Selected Poems and Letters*, edited and translated by Margaret Rosenthal and Ann Rosalind Jones

Lucrezia Marinella, *The Nobility and Excellence of Women*, edited and translated by Anne Dunhill

Antonia Pulci, *Florentine Drama for Convent and Festival*, annotated and translated by James Wyatt Cook

Anna Maria van Schurman, *Whether a Christian Woman Should Be Educated and Other Writings from Her Intellectual Circle*, edited and translated by Joyce Irwin

Arcangela Tarabotti, *Paternal Tyranny*, edited and translated by Letizia Panizza

INTRODUCTION

THE OTHER VOICE

Tullia d'Aragona, celebrated courtesan and poet, had her *Dialogue on the Infinity of Love* published in Venice by the well-known house of Giolito de' Ferrari in 1547. For a woman to enter the ongoing debate on human love was an unprecedented occurrence and, in cultural and social history, would be a unique event for centuries to come. In collections of short stories and in dialogues, women were depicted by men as participants in discussions on topical or philosophical subjects, but never before had a woman authored a work in which she cast herself as the main disputant on the ethics of love, a field exclusively in the male domain. Stated in Platonic and Aristotelian terminology, the definition of human love given by Aragona represents a significant deviation from the prevailing theories of her times: she posits no sublimation of eros, as the Platonists did, no forsaking of human passion in favor of an experience that can be called speculative or spiritual. Human beings are made of body and soul, sense and intellect. If a relationship between woman and man is to be lasting, she argues, it must be based on the real nature of humankind. Honorable love is therefore to be viewed in terms of both sensual and intellectual needs. Sexual drives are irrepressible and blameless, she maintains; they become immoral only when unrestrained by reason.

Certainly, Aragona's concept of love is fashioned from ideas and definitions current in sixteenth-century educated discourse, but the use she makes of them carries radical implications. By founding the male-female bond on nature, she establishes a new morality of love. By positing the parity between the sexes, she removes women, traditionally identified with physicality and sin, from the marginal position they occupied in men's progress to spiritual life and salvation and gives womanhood new meaning.

Aragona's work is very much the expression of her times. Trained to be a high-level courtesan in an affluent and tolerant society, throughout her life she faced the increasingly severe consequences of economic decline and the concerted plan by church and governments to do away with the ethical laxity that had prevailed in the first decades of the century. Seen in the background of this conservative backlash, the *Dialogue on the Infinity of Love* displays its true significance as the attempt on the part of a woman, who was sexually liberated and accustomed to economic independence, to fight back the forces that were restraining her freedom and denying her very sense of self.

BIOGRAPHY

Tullia d'Aragona was born in Rome around 1510. Her mother, Giulia Campana, was a courtesan from Adria, on the river Po, who exercised her profession during the papacy of Leo X, when educated courtesans were allowed great freedom of movement, consumption of wealth, and a good measure of prestige and admiration. Tullia's wedding certificate attests that she was the daughter of one Costanzo Palmieri d'Aragona, but Giulia let it be known that the father was an illustrious cardinal d'Aragona whom modern historians have assumed to be Luigi d'Aragona.[1] From Pietro Aretino we learn that she was trained as a *virtuosa* and that she spoke Tuscan from the time when, still a child, she resided in Siena with her mother.[2] Other contemporaries confirm that she read music, played the lute, and sang as well as composed her own verse. These skills were expected of *cortegiane honeste*, as well as court ladies, and made them favorite companions of literati, noblemen, and prelates; but, in addition, Aragona was known to possess a natural sharpness of intellect, presumably refined by a daily familiarity with intellectuals, and a remarkable ability to converse on a variety of difficult subjects.[3] From about 1535 to 1548, with her

1. According to a tradition going back to allusions made by Pietro Aretino in "Zoppino fatto frate e Ludovico puttaniere," written in 1534 (in *Ragionamenti* [Rome: Newton Compton, 1972], pp. 151–52), and by Girolamo Muzio in his eclogue "Tirrhenia" (in Aragona's *Le rime,* ed. E. Celani. Bologna, 1891, p. 189), Tullia's father was Luigi d'Aragona, natural son of Diana Guardato and Ferdinand I of Naples, who was made cardinal by pope Alessandro VI Borgia in 1493. See E. Celani's "Introduction" to *Le rime di Tullia d'Aragona* (Bologna: Romagnoli, 1891), pp. xx–xxxii, and S. Bongi, *Annali di Gabriel Giolito de' Ferrari* (Rome, 1890), 1:152.

2. "Zoppino fatto frate etc.," in *Ragionamenti,* p. 300. The word *virtuosa* indicates a trained professional, often a singer or musician, or an accomplished courtesan. Salvatore Battaglia defines the sixteenth-century *cortegiana* as a woman of refined upbringing and intellectual qualities who gives her sexual favors in a relation of mutual respect and esteem (*Grande Dizionario della Lingua Italiana* [Turin: UTET, 1971], 3:863).

3. A clear allusion to Aragona can be found in "Zoppino fatto frate etc.," where a courtesan is mentioned who can quote all Petrarch and Boccaccio by heart and innumerable lines from the Latin poets as well (Aretino, *Ragionamenti,* p. 298). For Aragona's musical and cultural accomplishments, see Battista Stambellino's letter to Isabella d'Este, dated 13 June 1537, published by

mother and retinue, she made a series of residential moves that took her to Adria, to Venice, Ferrara, Siena, and Florence. These travels were most likely an attempt to maintain the financial and social status to which Tullia and her mother had been accustomed and which was becoming precarious in one Italian state after another. These were also the years of increasing moral conservatism, when society was hit by a number of sumptuary laws and regulations aimed at sharply defining the categories of citizens and at limiting the visibility of courtesans.[4] It is not known for what reasons Aragona left Florence in 1548 and decided to return to Rome. Documents indicate that her circumstances declined progressively and that she died in March 1556 and was buried in the Roman church of Sant'Agostino. From her will we get a hint of her continued cultural interests. Among the household effects sold to local dealers there was a trunk containing thirteen books of music, about thirty-five Latin and Italian volumes on a variety of subjects and in various states of preservation, and a great many more books and papers in tattered condition, which, probably for that reason, were not specified in number and content.[5]

Aragona was in Venice around 1535. Although brief, her sojourn there contributed to establishing her reputation as the intellectual courtesan par excellence: it was her Venetian home that inspired the setting for Sperone Speroni's *Dialogue on Love*. One of the characters in this youthful and popular work is a courtesan named Tullia who outshines all of the other speakers in eloquence and fervor while upholding the view that passion and reason are mutually exclusive.[6]

In June 1437, Tullia was at Ferrara where the Este court, tolerant of new ideas and keen on cultural and pleasurable pursuits, attracted artists and literati from the rest of the peninsula. Here Aragona enjoyed a period of social success and met Girolamo Muzio (1496–1576). A soldier and a writer in the service of Duke Ercole II, Muzio became her lover, then eventually the editor of her dialogue and her long-standing publicity agent. As a writer, he showed his pragmatic character in the solutions he proposed to a great variety of moral and literary dilemmas. When institutional rigidity and human weakness made

---

Alessandro Luzio in *Rivista storica mantovana*, I (1885): 179. Aragona's intelligence and eloquence are praised in a variety of texts: by Jacopo Nardi in a letter accompanying his translation of Cicero's *Pro Marcello* that he sent to Gian Francesco della Stufa in 1536; by Niccolò Martelli in his letter to Aragona, dated 16 March 1546; by Alessandro Arrighi in his sonnet to her; and by Gerolamo Muzio in "Tirrhenia" (Bongi, *Annali*, pp. 163, 179; Aragona, *Rime*, pp. 117, 187).

4. On the change that the Sack of 1527 brought to the status of Roman courtesans and of Roman society in general, see Aretino's *Ragionamenti*, p. 303.

5. Bongi, *Annali*, pp. 193–95.

6. *Dialogo d'amore* (in *Trattatisti del Cinquecento*, ed. M. Pozzi [Milan-Naples: Ricciardi, 1978], 1:517, 527–28.

problems insoluble, he tended to look for a compromise. He argued, for instance, in favor of the concubinage of canons and ecclesiastical lawyers on economic, hygienic, and moral grounds. He thought it expedient to set down the rules for dueling, in a book that became a best-seller, even though in principle he disapproved of this increasingly widespread way of settling personal disputes.[7]

His passionate temperament and his love for Aragona inspired him to compose ten erotic songs, incongruously veiled in Platonic terminology, and seven eclogues, in which pastoral fiction is used to sing of her earthly beauty, her noble parentage, and her lovers, of whom a long list is provided.[8] Muzio's unabashed enhancement of Tullia's desirability met with the lady's approval, although it was emended by a few touches of her own. In a letter to Antonio Mezabarba, written in 1550, Muzio tells him that one day in Ferrara, after some thoughtful consideration, Tullia asked him to celebrate her under the name Talia rather than Tirrhenia, thus replacing a too-common pastoral fiction of nymph and shepherd with a more dignified literary allegory of the muse of idyllic verse and her poet. She also instructed Muzio to arrange the change in such a way as to make the connection between nymph and muse clear, lest the past celebration and publicity be in vain.[9]

A set of three documents preserved in the Archivio di Stato of Siena shows that Aragona was in that city in 1543, and that in 1544 she was denounced, and later excused, for not dressing in the fashion prescribed for courtesans.[10] Siena had fallen under the sphere of influence of the church and of the Emperor Charles V. New laws were regimenting the citizenry and endeavoring to regulate their lives within strictly enforced separation lines. From this time on, Aragona engaged in a struggle to preserve her image as a refined courtesan and secure for herself the social tolerance that had come with that image. After the

7. Muzio's views on concubinage are expressed in a verse epistle addressed to Andrea Ruperti and found in *Rime diverse* (Venice: Giolito, 1551), pp. 109r–110r. *Il duello* was published in Venice by Giolito in 1550 and had twelve editions by 1564, of which two were published in Lyon. Besides writing profusely on literary style and religious concerns, Muzio wrote books on conduct and manners such as *Le risposte cavalleresche* (Venice: Giolito, 1550), which saw fifteen editions by 1604; *Il gentiluomo* (Venice: Valvassore, 1464) and *Il cavaliero* (Rome: Blado, 1569), and two treatises on marriage. On the news of her wedding to one Silvestro Guicciardini, one of them, *Trattato di matrimonio*, was dedicated to Aragona.

8. Of Muzio's verse inspired by Aragona, the sonnets and canzoni were published in *Rime diverse* (Venice: Giolito, 1551) and the love eclogues in the first book of *Ecloghe* (Venice: Giolito, 1550).

9. Muzio's letter to Mezabarba is in *Delle lettere*, ed. Sermartelli (Florence, 1590; Rpt. ed. by L. Borsetto, Sala Bolognese: Forni, 1985), pp. 196–99.

10. S. Bongi, "Il velo giallo di Tullia d'Aragona" in *Rivista critica della letteratura italiana* 3, no. 3 (1886): 85–95.

fall of Siena's political regime, where she had found high-placed friends and protectors of sorts, and after her life and property were threatened, Aragona moved to Florence. New denunciations would follow her to Florence as well, but before they did she enjoyed the events that led her to publication and to lasting literary fame. By that time, she had gathered around a new circle of professional and amateur literati, and discussions were frequently held in her home on matters of current intellectual interest.[11] Benedetto Varchi and Lattanzio Benucci, who appear as speakers in her *Dialogue on the Infinity of Love*, were close friends and the most frequent participants in these gatherings.

During this time, Benedetto Varchi (1503–65) was the most influential man of letters in Florence. In philosophy he professed to be an Aristotelian, although he was inclined toward many Platonic ideas, especially on the subject of love. A Florentine, he had a natural talent for the local idiom and subscribed enthusiastically, and often pedantically, to Bembo's idea that the literary language for all Italians ought to be based on Petrarch's *Canzoniere* and Boccaccio's *Decameron*. For these reasons, he admirably fitted Duke Cosimo's plan for the linguistic and cultural hegemony of Florence over the rest of Italy, and, after acquiring a dominant position at the Accademia Fiorentina, he began to exercise his sway over the literary scene and act as the cultural mediator between the duchy and other learned centers. It is no surprise then if, as A. Racheli states, many contemporary writers, among them Aragona, paid homage to Varchi and, following a widespread custom among literati, sent some of their writings for his approval and corrections.[12]

Varchi probably met Tullia at the end of 1546. By that time he had written a good quantity of verse and had lectured on philosophical topics at the Accademia degli Infiammati of Padua and at the Accademia Fiorentina, but the bulk of his lectures was delivered after his friendship with Aragona had come to an end. Of Tullia's correspondence with Varchi only eight letters have survived. They corroborate the dialogue in showing a comfortable familiarity between them and a mutual understanding for the difficulties that both suffered at the hands of their enemies. Most of these missives speak of sonnets being exchanged, but only one brief mention is made of the dialogue: "From time to

11. In *Ercolano*, written late in life, Varchi refers to a debate that took place in Tullia's house, with Muzio present, on the correct use of the Tuscan language and on whether a non-Tuscan would be capable of it (*Opere* [Trieste, 1859], 2:75).

12. A. Racheli's statement can be found on p. XIV of "Della filologia del secolo XVI e in particolare della vita e degli scritti di Benedetto Varchi," which is the introduction to Varchi's *Opere*. For Varchi's Aristotelianism, see Bruno Nardi in *Studi su Pietro Pomponazzi* (Florence: Le Monnier, 1965), pp. 322–28, and Umberto Pirotti in *Benedetto Varchi e la cultura del suo tempo* (Florence: Olschki, 1971), pp. 78–108. For Cosimo's cultural plan, see again Pirotti, p. 21. Varchi's poems were first published in 1555 and 1557; now they can be read in *Opere*, 2:831–1016.

time, do converse with my dialogue," urges Tullia in her letter of 25 August 1546. The letter proves that her interest in the subject of love predates her denunciation to the Florentine authorities and that her work had been completed before an impelling need arose to prove her legitimacy as a writer.[13]

Soon after a new sumptuary law was promulgated on 19 October 1546, Tullia was summoned by the authorities for not complying with the regulation obliging courtesans to wear a yellow cover when in public. Varchi, who had been trained as a lawyer and acted as the legal advisor to a number of powerful men, helped Tullia to word the petition to the duchess Eleonora which asked for an exemption. The Archivio di Stato of Florence has preserved the document on which Cosimo penned the notation "to be exonerated in consideration of her being a poet," together with the deliberation by the Signori Luogotenenti et Consiglieri, dated 1 May 1547, granting the exemption on the grounds of Aragona's "rare knowledge of poetry and philosophy."[14]

A few months later, Tullia's lyric poetry came out in print. Her dialogue on love was consigned to Muzio on his way to Venice in October. It was published there before the end of the same year with a prefatory letter by Muzio, followed by Aragona's dedication to Cosimo. In this translation, Muzio's letter, which in the modern edition appears in the appendix, has been restored to its original position. The success of the dialogue was marked by a second edition by Giolito in 1552. The next edition was brought out in Naples by Antonio Bulifon in 1694. Eugenio Camerini saw to the first publication of modern times (Milan: G. Daelli, 1864), and a reprint was made of it by A. Forni in 1974. The critical edition, on which the present translation is based, was prepared by Giuseppe Zonta in 1912 and included in his collection of sixteenth-century dialogues on love, *Trattati d'amore del Cinquecento*, a volume in the Laterza series of Italian classics. It was reprinted and edited by Mario Pozzi in 1975 and 1980.

Aragona's publications were duly registered by compilers of literary encyclopedias and by eighteenth-century historians, such as Crescimbeni, Quadrio and Tiraboschi, who were the first to gather documentary evidence of cultural activity in Italy. The literary histories written soon after the unification of the country in 1860 regarded the Cinquecento literature, especially the literature on love, an expression of the moral decadence of the nation. On Aragona, furthermore, weighed heavily the stigma of prostitution, which, in

13. Aragona's letters to Varchi were published by Guido Biagi in "Un'etera romana. Tullia d'Aragona," in *Nuova Antologia*, series III, vol. 4, no. 16 (1886): 655–711. The dialogue is mentioned in the letter dated 25 August 1546, on p. 697.

14. Petition and deliberation can be read in Bongi, *Annali*, pp. 184–85, and in his "Il velo giallo. . . .," pp. 89–90.

her case, seemed to besmirch what was considered the noble pursuit of literary studies. In the nineteenth century, full credit of authorship was questioned for Aragona, as was often the case with women authors from classical antiquity to the Renaissance. At the same time, her publications were regarded by some as an attempt to gloss over a vicious life and a shameful profession.[15]

Contrary to such anachronistic assumptions, Aragona exhibited a strong sense of personal worth and took a detailed interest in shaping her image as a refined and glamorous courtesan. In later life, she used her intellectual talents to carve a social and psychological space against what was for her a mounting tide of oppressive regulations. The publication of her writings may well have been hastened by the necessity of defending her claim to a higher social status, but her contribution to the ongoing debate on love is of original import. To appreciate fully its fundamental assumptions, her dialogue needs to be read in the context of contemporary discourse and with a view to the value system implied by that discourse.[16]

ANTECEDENTS

Many treatises on love published or written in the early 1500s draw their basic tenets from Marsilio Ficino's theory of "Platonic love." Ficino's philosophy had been made accessible to a large public by his Latin commentary on Plato's *Symposium*, which the author himself translated into Italian in 1474. Working at the height of the humanistic revival, Ficino proposed a version of Platonism harmonious with Christianity and with the humanistic concept of humankind at the center of creation. Love is the universal force binding the world and the divinity together, for God has created the world and governs it through an act of love, and through love the world returns to the godhead. Similarly the human soul follows an itinerary that goes from love of earthly beauty to the ecstatic contemplation of the divine.[17]

The many subsequent popularizations of Platonic love, almost all written

15. The credit due to Aragona for this work is implicitly reduced by the scholars who believe the dialogue to be the faithful transcription of a conversation. Even so, the question of authorship was settled favorably by Aragona's modern editor, Giuseppe Zonta, in *Trattati d'amore del Cinquecento* (Bari: Laterza, 1912), pp. 360–62. Cf. p. 63, footnote 12 to the dialogue.

16. For a survey of criticism and bibliography on Aragona, see Rinaldina Russell, "Tullia d'Aragona," in *Italian Women Writers*, ed. R. Russell. Westport, CT: Greenwood, 1994, pp. 31–33. For Girolamo Tiraboschi, see his *Storia della letteratura italiana* (Florence: Molini Landi, 1812), 7:1172.

17. Marsilio Ficino, *Commentarium in Convivium Platonis de Amore*, in *Marsili Florentini . . . Opera et quae hactenus extitere* (Basileae, 1561), 5:1320–63. It was translated into Italian by Ficino and was published in Florence in 1544 as *Sopra lo amore o ver' Convito di Platone*. Sears Jayne has provided an English translation in *Commentary on Plato's "Symposium" on Love* (Dallas, TX: Spring Publications, 1985).

in dialogic form, indicate that a large reading public was concerned with human dilemmas and with the relation of sensual experience to reason and to religious morality. They responded to the need, very much felt by the intellectual class, of bridging the gulf between secular and religious values, between private conduct and the moral and spiritual discipline that the church idealized. The dialogue was the genre most apt to negotiate this conflict, for it proposed as worthy of investigation many possible solutions, thus minimizing the contrast between irreconcilable positions. It afforded the civilized custom of sharing consonant opinions, while providing the vicarious pleasure of interesting conversation, often with characters who represented well-known people.[18]

The first dialogue on love in the vernacular was *Gli Asolani* (1505), by the Venetian nobleman and, later, Cardinal Pietro Bembo.[19] It simulated a conversation between ladies and gentlemen in the small northern court of Asolo, which the Venetian republic had assigned to Caterina Corner (Cornaro in modern Tuscanized form). It responded to the question: which is the form of love that does not endanger the moral well-being of the lovers? Different solutions are considered in turn by three speakers. To Perottino's oration on the destructive perturbations of human passion, succeeds Gismondo's warm eulogy of the sweet pleasures of love, both those of the lower senses, to be indulged in sparingly, and those afforded by the "spiritual" senses of sight and hearing. Love affords many delights to the temperate lover, maintains Gismondo, and is the source of all the good that nature contains. It makes friendship and society possible and promotes civility.

The third speaker, Lavinello, considers a fundamental distinction between natural love and human love. Natural love is instinctive and innocent, but human love must always be responsible, for it is negotiated by reason and by the individual's unavoidable exercise of free will. The last word on love, however, seems to be left to a strict Christian spokesman. A holy hermit's authority is, at the end, brought into the Asolo conversations to argue that the only kind of love worthy of man is love for God and that any form of human attachment is an obstacle in man's progress to salvation and heavenly bliss. Bem-

18. The bibliography on the sixteenth-century dialogue is vast. A good introduction are John McClelland's "Dialogue et Rhétorique à la Renaissance," in *Le Dialogue*, ed. P. R. Léon and P. Perron (Ottawa: Didier, 1985), pp. 157–64, and Peter Burke's "The Renaissance Dialogue," in *Renaissance Studies* 3, no. 1, (1989): 1–12. The most extensive treatment of the genre undertaken to date is Virginia Cox's *The Renaissance Dialogue: Literary Dialogue in its Social and Political Contexts, Castiglione to Galileo* (Cambridge: Cambridge University Press, 1992).

19. Pietro Bembo, *Gli Asolani*, trans. Rudolf B. Gottfried. (Bloomington: Indiana University Press, 1954).

bo does not resolve the dilemma of his characters' contrasting views. Rather, by offering a number of solutions as all worthy of investigation, he reaches an amiable compromise. His refined consideration of many types of human feeling, and their possible social outlets, found a receptive welcome in the higher strata of society and among their literati. It also started a trend toward the depiction of an idealized court life in literature and the arts.

No sixteenth-century work demonstrates this idealization better than Baldesar Castiglione's *The Book of the Courtier* with its description of the perfect courtier and the accomplished court lady. The significance of this book is in the proof it provides that the limits of men's experience had expanded beyond the traditional pursuit of war, politics, or asceticism.[20] For women, its importance consists in having officially sanctioned the female presence in the male world by gracing that presence with the social and moral qualities that the aristocracy had come to value. In its last section, Pietro Bembo, Castiglione's friend and one of the book's characters, is chosen to declaim on Platonic love as the only form of love becoming the dignified status of a man at court. With a poetic legerdemain, the Bembo character creates a continuous progression from love of earthly beauty to love of God, making man's feeling for a woman the first stage in the arduous ascent to transcendence. In imitation of this aristocratic view of human relationships, it henceforth became a literary commonplace to represent the bond between woman and man in the terms and the guises supplied by Platonic love.

In circulation, however, there were already treatises that presented a more realistic view of life and dealt sympathetically with human sexuality. Even in his predominantly Platonic *Book on the Nature of Love*, begun in 1495 and published in Mantua in 1525, Mario Equicola had stated that whoever loves permanently must love the body as well as the soul, because the nature of love requires that not only the lovers' souls be loved, but that their senses too be satisfied in their natural need for sensual pleasure.[21] In Agostino Nifo's *On Beauty and Love* (1531), love is a condition brought about by the sensual appetite ("affectus appetitus sensitivi") and the beautiful is defined as what moves the soul through the senses and impels human beings to a bodily fruition, which is achieved through the sense of touch and in sexual intercourse.[22]

20. Baldesar Castiglione, *The Book of the Courtier*. Trans. with an introduction by George Bull (Hammondsworth, Middlesex, England: Penguin Books, 1984).

21. Mario Equicola, *D'Alveto di Natura d'amore* (Venice: Giolito de' Ferrari, 1563), p. 381.

22. Agostino Nifo, *De pulchro et amore* (Rome: A. Blado, 1531). To sexual attractions, Nifo adds the pleasure provided by intellectual accomplishments and gracious manners and enjoyed by sight and hearing. These were the "virtues" expected of a *cortegiana honesta*. Cfr. Benedetto Croce, "Il *De Pulchro* di Agostino Nifo," in *Poeti e scrittori del pieno e tardo Rinascimento* (Bari: Laterza, 1952), 3:105.

For the writers of the generation after Bembo the most authoritative claim for the pleasure and the goodness of the sexual union was to be found in Leone Ebreo's *Dialogues on Love* (1535). This is the work that supplied Aragona with the terminology, the concepts, and some of the arguments leading to her definition of love. In universal terms, love is described by Leone as a force uniting the created world to God in a harmonious circularity. At the center of the universe is the human being, a microcosm made of matter and spirit, whose dual nature reflects the mutual correspondence of heaven and earth and makes the connection between the spiritual and the corporeal realms possible. In human terms, perfect love is one that correspondingly yearns for the union of both body and soul, for a physical consummation that confirms and strengthens the spiritual union already brought about by reason and by the higher senses.[23]

Among the works in which traces of Leone's vindication of sexuality can easily be detected, three were published a few years before or at the same time as Aragona's work: Sperone Speroni's *Dialogue on Love* (1542), Giuseppe Betussi's *Raverta* (1544), and Francesco Sansovino's *Conversation Whereby Young People Are Taught the Fine Art of Loving* (1545).[24] Sansovino's *Conversation* is a commonsense *ars amandi* in which some Ovidian ideas are adapted to the possibilities of sixteenth-century youths. It contains a criticism of homophilia which may well have been in Aragona's mind when she wrote her passage on the subject.[25] In Giuseppe Betussi's *Raverta*, Raverta, the main speaker, gives to the inquiring courtesan and poet Francesca Baffa a definition of love that is of the Platonic kind. Even so, he maintains that incorporeal beauty can be imagined only after viewing material objects. Moreover, to Baffa's contention that the body is made superfluous in the mind's ascent to higher forms of contemplation, Raverta argues that the body is in effect essential to the attainment of a superior form of love, for only the senses make cognition possible.[26]

An even greater consideration for natural instincts is found in Sperone Speroni's *Dialogue on Love*. When the character Grazia celebrates the dual nature of man and of love, he clearly is following the epistemological footsteps of Pietro Pomponazzi, the eminent Aristotelian philosopher whose classes

---

23. *Dialoghi d'amore*, ed. S. Caramella (Bari: Laterza, 1929), pp. 50–51.

24. Cfr. Nesca A. Robb, *Neoplatonism of the Italian Renaissance* (New York: Octagon Books, 1968; reprint of London: George Allen and Unwin Ltd., 1935), p. 203, and Robert Ellrodt, *Neoplatonism in the Poetry of Spenser* (Genève: E. Droz, 1960), pp. 145–46.

25. "If their love were truly love of contemplation, the Platonists would love mature men rather than young and immature ones," argues Sansovino in his *Ragionamento nel quale brevemente si insegna ai giovani la bella arte d'amore* (1545), now in *Trattati d'amore del Cinquecento*, p. 165.

26. *Trattati d'amore del Cinquecento*, pp. 17, 19 and 32.

Speroni had attended in Bologna. Love, Grazia maintains, is an affection born in the senses and shaped by reason. Lovers, dissatisfied with only being able to see and hear their beloveds, endeavor as much as they can to pleasure the other senses too. And when the pleasure of the mind is added to those of senses, the "amorous hermaphrodite," that is, the perfect union between man and woman, is truly achieved.[27]

Such statements about sensory perception can be considered the great divide between Platonic and Aristotelian concepts of love, for they have far-reaching implications into epistemological theory.[28] For Ficino and his followers, knowledge comes not from experience but from within the soul, where all universal forms are buried. The contemplation of these forms can be obtained by the human mind when it separates itself from the life of the body and from sensory impressions. Consequently, in their theory of love, the Platonists draw a dividing line between the lower senses—touch, smell, and taste, which perform the bodily functions—and the senses of hearing, sight, and reason, which are considered spiritual because they are capable of perceiving things of a spiritual nature. In this view, human love is a hindrance to the contemplation of the pure form that is God, as the holy hermit in Bembo's *Gli Asolani* and the Bembo character in Castiglione's *The Courtier* declare. Man must ultimately be rid of all human attachments, no matter how spiritual they are deemed, if he is to achieve the purity of vision that alone can direct his soul to the godhead.

For the Aristotelians, on the other hand, the human mind has no direct knowledge of ideas, and cognition proceeds from sense perception and from experience. According to Pietro Pomponazzi, man's soul is in constant need of sensory perceptions, and there is nothing to be found in man's mind that was not in his senses before.

While Platonism flourished at the courts, including the most powerful of them, the Roman court, Aristotelian philosophy and its method of "scientific" analysis were prevalent in the northern university centers, such as Padua and Bologna. And between these towns and the prosperous press industry of Venice, a new type of literary man circulated, of independent mind and means. Such were Betussi, Sansovino, Speroni, Muzio and, to a degree, Varchi.

There are indications that some of these authors were aware of the difference in the social backgrounds favoring the two ideologies of human behav-

27. Ibid., p. 517.

28. About sensory perceptions, see Pietro Pomponazzi, "On the Immortality of the Soul, *"Renaissance Philosophy of Man*, ed. E. Cassirer, P. O. Kristeller, J. H. Randall, Jr. (Chicago: Chicago University Press, 1965), pp. 272–73, 287, 305. See also Bruno Nardi, *Studi su Pietro Pomponazzi* (Florence: Le Monnier, 1965), pp. 33–34, 42.

ior.[29] Betussi suggests that the ideal of spiritual love is not valid for all categories of people. In *Raverta* a distinction is made between "wise men" and "ordinary men," the latter being members of an aristocratic class to which the author seems to attribute the willingness to exercise the self-control that is a prerequisite of meditation and asceticism.[30] In Speroni's *Dialogue on Love*, the Grazia character obviously has the Platonists in mind when arguing against those who think it possible to gratify their intellectual needs and disregard all sensual appetites—as if swallowing their food without chewing it—thereby doing harm to themselves.[31] It is to the courtesan Tullia that Speroni assigns the task of satirizing the Bembian view of love. Launching into her passionate eulogy of eroticism, Tullia draws support from some witty narratives about the origins and phenomenology of love, which have lewd overtones and are a parody of well-known Platonic myths. And, just as Lavinello quotes the holy hermit in *Gli Asolani* and Socrates quotes Diotima in *Symposium*, she appeals to the authority of Francesco Maria Molza, a poet renowned for his sense of humor, erotic *novelle*, and profligate life-style.

Significantly, Betussi's and Speroni's dialogues have a courtesan as one of their speakers. The prominent placement of a courtesan is surely a sign that a discussion on natural love and sexuality was understood to fall within the purview of a specific category of femininity. And this category was conceived, and its representative—Speroni's Tullia—described, in line with the accepted view of womanhood and of love. Aragona's dialogue is the answer of a woman, a *virtuosa* of love, who disputes the adequacy of both the spiritualistic and sensualistic views of love and who is ready to argue with men over the difference between making love and being in love.

THE DIALOGUE

The dialogue represents a discussion taking place among friends at the Florentine quarters of Tullia d'Aragona in 1547. Benedetto Varchi has just arrived, interrupting a conversation among Tullia, Doctor Lattanzio Benucci, and other men. Varchi is afraid of disturbing them, but is reassured that he is welcome. Indeed, they were waiting for him to arrive and solve an important question: can love be endless, or does one always love within bounds? It is Tul-

29. Marcello Aurigemma, *Lirica, poemi e trattati civili del Cinquecento* (Rome-Bari: Laterza, 1973), pp. 41–48. For the same period in Italian literary history, see Carlo Dionisotti, "Letteratura Italiana nell'età del Concilio di Trento," *Geografia e storia della letteratura italiana* (Turin: Einaudi, 1967), pp. 183–204.

30. In *Trattati d'amore del Cinquecento*, pp. 30–31.

31. In *Trattatisti del Cinquecento*, 1:517.

lia's turn to speak; is perhaps Signor Varchi reluctant to engage in an argument with a woman?, she teasingly asks, for she has heard of some "philosophical" reasons Varchi holds on women's inferiority.

On this note of feminine challenge, the discussion begins at once and proceeds like a casual conversation by fits and starts, interruptions and digressions. Various themes intertwine apparently at random, always starting a new argument and preventing the previous one from reaching a linear conclusion. The debate is kept lively by a continuous flow of playful repartees and asides, of feigned ignorance and spirited retorts on Tullia's part. But this is no aimless imitation of life, for the seemingly casual conversation is orchestrated toward the solution of the main question. In the apparent discontinuity, contradictions and flaws are found in the working definitions, more precise terms are proposed, and corollaries to the main theory are established. All topics are in the end justified and made to fit the conclusion desired by the author.

There are three speakers in the dialogue: Tullia d'Aragona, who acts as the master of ceremonies, directing and concluding the discussion; Benedetto Varchi, who provides the dialogue with the appropriate philosophical garb; and Doctor Benucci, who, after the main question has been debated, reports on the conversants' previous discussion. Repeated mention is made of the presence of an unspecified number of gentlemen. These reminders, as well as the reference to other known people who might chance to come by, add to the verisimilitude of the situation.

The main focus of the discussion concerns the infinity of love. Varchi is bent on the scholastic method of debating the question following a preordained sequence.[32] With idiosyncratic punctiliousness, he insists on a definition of all terms used: is "end" the same as "aim," and is "love" the same as "to love"? This leads to a number of digressions—on substance and accident, matter and form, causation and infinity, among others—and to arguments that tend to turn on themselves. The first premise of Varchi's argument is based on the equivocation caused by the word *fine*, which means both "cessation" and "goal." The second is offered by Tullia's preliminary definition of "love" and of "to love." Love, she declares, is a desire to enjoy with union what is beautiful or seems beautiful to the lover. And "to love" is to desire that union. So, if "end" is the same as "aim," and "love" is in essence the same as "to love," then love, Varchi is swift to conclude, is without end.

Such deductive wizardry fails to persuade Signora Tullia, and Varchi

---

32. The "questio" was a literary genre patterned on the *disputatio*, that is to say, on the discussion of a proposed thesis, a custom that was practiced in the universities where the Aristotelian tradition was still strong. See P. O. Kristeller, "The Aristotelian Tradition," *Renaissance Thought*, 1:31.

turns the question around: what proofs does she have that love comes to an end? I have no proof, she replies, but experience shows me that men, having made love, forsake their women and stop loving. Empirical observation notwithstanding, Varchi goes on arguing syllogistically that love is infinite, because whoever loves, when loving, loves without end in sight, and when he stops loving, the question no longer pertains. Needless to say, Tullia remains unconvinced. She will, therefore, take up the questioning herself and, in Socratic fashion, reduce his logically argued position to absurdity.

She begins by reminding Varchi of the Aristotelian principle, much vaunted by him, that there is no such thing as infinity: so, how can love be infinite? The dilemma is removed by a long digression that distinguishes between actual and potential infinity. Love is infinite potentially, not in actuality, for lovers' desires are endless and can never be fully satisfied by anything at all. After obtaining one thing, they want something else, and something else again and again, and so on *ad infinitum*. Here Varchi, forever faithful to his scholastic method, puts forward a counterargument. All moving objects are moved by an outside force or end, as Aristotle teaches, and no longer move when they have reached that end. In the same way, lovers, who all have a goal, no longer love when their goal is achieved and their desire satisfied.

Tullia is very grateful that there is such an extraordinary thing as logic, for, by demonstrating in turn the correctness of two opposite views—that love is infinite and that love is not infinite—it has helped her to advance toward her conclusion. The solution lies again in the meaning given to the equivocal term "love." One must differentiate between two types of love: "vulgar" love and "honest" love. Vulgar love comes quickly to an end because it is directed exclusively to the pleasure of the flesh and ceases when the object of desire is attained. It often turns into hatred and disgust. Honest love, on the other hand, fosters in itself a continuity of affection. Since human nature partakes of both matter and intellect, perfect lovers must indeed long for a union of both body and soul. Their spiritual coming together is possible, but a perfect physical union can never be attained, for bodies do not penetrate into each other's space. Honest love is therefore by its very nature endless, for it is destined to yearn endlessly for that perfect consummation that can never be experienced.

After the discussion on love's infinity, three short queries are advanced by Varchi, which prove to be corollaries to the main thesis. Two of these questions—is natural love to be considered immoral? and why is it that some lovers love more passionately after the physical conquest?—turn on the same fundamental assumption about human nature: human beings are made of two contrasting elements, matter and intellect. Natural love is innocent. Only an incontinent use of sensual resources is morally condemnable, as are those lovers who are attracted exclusively to their beloveds' bodies and wish to indulge in repeated copulation.

The third query is what is to be thought of the love of men for men? Sexual intercourse between men is immediately and perfunctorily dismissed as sinful by both speakers. But if homosexual love is sinful, presses Tullia, why did Plato praise it? And, if Phaedrus' and Alcibiades' speeches are to be read, as Varchi contends, as eulogies on philosophical love, why is it, she continues, that women are excluded from it? Varchi—who in real life found himself on more than one occasion in the position of having to justify his love for young male pupils as being philosophical in nature—is here made to face a contradiction that cannot be undone syllogistically: Platonic love seems to idealize women while at the same time marginalizing them as intellectually inferior and thus incapable of spiritual relationships. Tullia's interest is not in condemning homophilia, but rather in probing the misogynistic nature of Platonic love and in using that very bias to expose the element of sensuality that exists even in a category of love that professes to be purely spiritual in nature.

When all side issues are satisfactorily settled, Varchi is apprised of the subjects discussed by the company prior to his arrival on the scene. The dialogue closes with a praise of Aragona and her friends and admirers.

ANALYSIS OF THE DIALOGUE

In its sources, the *Dialogue on the Infinity of Love* presents a confluence of the Aristotelian and the Platonic traditions. While many terms and definitions are supplied by the schools (via Varchi), the main question and some secondary themes are derived from the vernacular literature on love. However, Aragona's discussion is closer in intent to those writings that present alternative views to the Bembian categorization of human affections.

For the basic principles of love, Aragona draws directly from Leone Ebreo. Her general definition is a near paraphrase of Leone's: "love is a desire to enjoy and to be united with what is either beautiful or seems beautiful to the lover." More significant are her transposition of Leone's concept of perfect human love and the emphasis she places on it. Good love, Aragona maintains, love generated by reason, that is, by the knowledge of the beloved's good qualities, yearns for spiritual and physical fulfillment. Set apart from vulgar love, which ceases when the desire for carnal pleasure is satisfied, honorable love is not brought to an end by copulation. On the contrary, its permanency is guaranteed by the very quality of desire, which is a yearning for the union of both body and soul—a yearning as insuppressible as it is impossible to satisfy.

Such a definition clearly challenges the validity of the erotic model upheld by Bembo's followers. Since in human affections the impulse toward sensuality cannot be totally removed, a love that purports to be purely spiritual is a travesty of human nature, outside the realm of human possibilities. This model is dismissed by Tullia who heaps on its eulogists and purported practitioners a hyperbolic praise that reaches for the unbelievably sublime. "It is hard to find enough praise," she states, "for anyone who rises by way of divine love from the human plane to that of immortal gods. . . . For my part," she goes on, "I can never read the words of that saintly hermit without feeling myself somehow elevated from the ground and transported to the heavens amidst such sweet sounds and ineffable chants, such rejoicing and bewilderment, that I can't explain the experience, nor could anyone else believe it if they had not experienced it."

While distancing herself from Platonic theory, Aragona abjures the opinions attributed to her in Speroni's *Dialogue on Love*. The character created by Speroni is an intelligent and articulate woman, but unmistakably a courtesan as seen by Speroni, unrestrained in her loves and ever-resurging jealousy, passionately inspired in her celebration of the irrational and deterministic essence of passion. Such a character would have found a tolerant public in the moral climate of earlier times and did reflect the bohemian mentality of some intellectual circles in the 1530s. In 1547, however, the increasingly censorial mood of officialdom had changed society, and Aragona saw fit to disavow the personality and values of Speroni's courtesan. Marshaling her own views and experience of human relationships, she proposes instead a bond of love, grounded in reason and by reason made consonant with nature and morality. The image that she wants to give of herself now is that of an "honorable" courtesan, restrained by wisdom in private life and concerned with social propriety in her literary endeavors. At the same time, she depicts her male friends as dignified gentlemen, interacting with quasi-Olympian reasonableness and with a reciprocity of love unsullied by jealousy, that mark of violent passion that engulfed Speroni's bohemian lovers.

What makes Aragona's position unprecedented, however, as well as unsurpassed by subsequent writers, is her linking the discussion of love and sex to gender issues. Aragona keeps her readers aware of the ongoing debate about women by repeated allusions that only seem to be tangential to the ongoing conversation. Varchi expresses several current prejudices about the female sex. He protests that in discussions and conversations women always argue irrationally. He also advances the opinion, often debated in his times, that women have no aptitude for love. At one point, in order to appease his interlocutor, he throws in the Platonic belief that women can exercise great power over men through their spiritual qualities and the beauty of their bodies. But Tullia will have none of all his clichés.

Aragona's ideas about gender are more sharply focused. To start with, we are made to understand that, in her opinion, many women possess higher moral qualities than do a host of men. As to the complaints vented by poets about their beloveds, the general perception of men's and women's relative merits would be different, Tullia maintains, if women, instead of men, were to write about them. More significantly, before and after the debate on love's infinity, Tullia raises two fundamental issues of gender bias, and by doing so she gives a radical turn to her theory of love.

Soon after his arrival on the scene, Tullia chides Varchi about his philosophical reasons for believing that women are not the equal of men. These "reasons," we may reasonably assume, refer to the statements contained in the lecture on human nature that the real Varchi had delivered in the Florentine Academy in the early part of 1547. Drawing from Aristotle, he pointed out the passive role played by women in procreation, implicitly restating their physical and moral inadequacy. In the same lecture, women's mental inferiority, thus their natural subordination to men, was used as an analogue to the subjugation of brute animals by intelligent human beings.[33]

Plato's gender bias, on the other hand, is exposed by Tullia when she calls into question the nature of love of men for boys. Her persistent questioning points out the truth about "Socratic" love: that the pedagogical and moral properties attributed to it are denied to the relation between woman and man because of women's supposed innate mental inferiority. In Plato's *Symposium*, Pausanias' speech distinguishes between a baser kind of love that can be directed to women and men alike, and a nobler kind, inspired by intelligence and vigor, which can therefore be addressed only to men.[34]

The view of women as the weak sex was given a scientific basis by Aristotle, who thus provided the justification for women's secondary position in the family, in society, and in the law. Being mentally weak, and consequently inca-

33. "Lezione sul Dante. Sulla generazione del corpo umano," *Opere*, 2:294a, 298–99b, 310a. See also p. 56, footnote 4.

34. *Symposium*, 181–181d. The question of Plato's feminism or antifeminism has been debated at length and mostly with respect to his political theory. See M. B. Arthur, "Early Greece: The Origins of the Western Attitude Toward Women," *Arethusa* 6 (1973): 7–58; D. Wender, "Plato: Misogynist, Paedophile, and Feminist," *Arethusa* 6 (1973): 75–90; S. B. Pomeroy, "Feminism in Book V of Plato's *Republic*," *Apeiron* 8 (1974): 32–35; J. J. Hannas "Plato's Republic and Feminism," *Philosophy* 51 (1976): 307–21; H. Lesser, "Plato's Feminism," *Philosophy* 54 (1979): 113–17; U. Mattioli, ἀσθένεια e ἀνδρεία. *Aspetti della femminilità nella letteratura classica, biblica e cristiana* (Rome: Bulzoni, 1983), pp. 13–17; E. Cantarella, *Pandora's Daughters: The Role and Status of Women in Greek and Roman Antiquity*, trans. M. B. Fant. (Baltimore: the Johns Hopkins University Press, 1981), pp. 58–59.

pable of controlling their own nature, women cannot be left in charge of themselves.[35] This concept of women's inferiority, typical of classical antiquity, was passed on to the church fathers who applied it to the interpretation of Genesis: it was Eve's natural weakness that allowed her to succumb to temptation, incite Adam to sin, and thereby cause the fall of humanity out of grace.[36] In the Renaissance notion of spiritual love, a distinction of essence is implied between male and female. Unsurprisingly then, the treatises on love that followed Ficino's line of thought, while praising earthly beauty, attributed to it and to woman a role that was only transitory. For in the Platonic ladder of love, woman represents the enticements of the senses that are to be foregone when time comes for replacing human affections with love for God.

Rather than proposing the gender issue for discussion, Aragona takes for granted that no reasonable man would want to doubt the essential equality of men and women. In this assumption, she was in tune with the most advanced views of some of her contemporaries. While more traditional treatises on the subject implied women's moral inferiority, even when they aimed at showing, by exemplification, that exceptions are possible, there were, nonetheless, new texts in circulation that argued in principle for women's equality. Mario Equicola's *On Women* (1501), Galeazzo Flavio Capra's *On the Excellence and Dignity of Women*, (1525) and Henricus Cornelius Agrippa's *The Nobility and Preeminence of the Female Sex*, whose Italian version became available as recently as 1544, all advanced the view that women's inferior position in society was not natural, but rather was due to men's tyranny and maintained by law, custom, and by the low-quality education given to girls.[37]

By standing on this side of the question, Aragona is able to call the bluff of Platonic theories and contest the Aristotelian notion of women's inferiority. The equality of the sexes is implied throughout the dialogue and is upheld by Tullia at crucial points. Her definition of honest love presumes the intellectual

---

35. In *De generatione animalium* Aristotle maintains that woman's procreative role is passive and that, with his sperm, man activates the matter in her and gives it form (728a). In *Politics* (IA, 5, 1254b or III, 1277b; III, 1260a) and in *Nichomachean Ethics* (VI, 2, 1139a12; VIII, 1162a) to women's natural physiological inferiority, he adds a mental and moral weakness. As their *bouleutikón* is fragile, that is, *àkuron*, they lack the necessary strength to be in charge of themselves, cannot control their lustful side, and are in need of male supervision. Cfr. Mattioli 16 and Cantarella 60.

36. *Genesis* 3, 15. See Ian MacLean, *The Renaissance Notion of Woman* (Cambridge: Cambridge University Press, 1980), pp. 16–17.

37. Mario Equicola, *De Mulieribus ad D. Margaritam Cantelmam* (Mantua, 1501), pp. a2r–a3r, a3v–a5v. Cf. Conor Fahy, "Three Early Renaissance Treatises on Women," *Italian Studies* XI (1956): 36–38. Galeazzo Flavio Capra. *Della eccellenza e dignità delle donne* (Rome, 1525; Ed. Maria Luisa Doglio, Rome, 1988), pp. 65, 106; Henricus Cornelius Agrippa, *The Nobility and Preeminence of the Female Sex*, ed. Albert Rabil, Jr. (Chicago: Chicago University Press, 1996), pp. 94–95.

and sexual equality of women and men. By advocating a kind of love that partakes of the intellectual and the sensual faculties of both lovers, Aragona implicitly argues for women's capacity for intellectual discourse and for their equal participation in the joyous life of the senses. The female sex is thus freed from the bondage to the physical side of human nature where it had been relegated by the theories that viewed women as the passive objects of male procreative sexuality. The male-female relationship that she proposes finds in itself the basis of its morality and is therefore independent of marriage and religious discipline.

Aragona's deviation from the prevailing theories of love is negotiated by a strategy of suggestions and statements directed to the reader and skillfully distributed between the frame of the dialogue and the structure of the debate proper. The characters, present as well as absent from the scene of the discussion, are well-known literary figures. Their coming together is referred to during the discussion, incidentally, as it were. In this way, an illusion is created of listening to an actual conversation, and it is maintained throughout by repeated reference to events pertaining to the real persons impersonated by the speakers. Even so, Aragona makes a very qualified use of the authority accruing to her discussion from the fame of her historical characters.

Signs of her attitude toward reigning authorities are given repeatedly. Aragona believes that one must trust reason, not authority. "I want you to bow to experience," Tullia says to Varchi. "I trust it by itself far more than the reasons produced by the whole class of philosophers!" She will accept authority only if validated by her own judgment, that is, "her understanding of it." She endorses freedom of thought: "let people judge for themselves and speak their opinion freely."

Sperone Speroni is highly commended, but his views of Aragona are rectified. Pietro Bembo's *Gli Asolani* gives proof of miraculous eloquence and great doctrine, but his theory of love is not praised. The eulogy for this most revered literary authority is *ad personam* and is lavish only on the surface. Varchi loves him for his virtues and his goodness. Tullia believes that "he retains a breed of nobility that the common herd readily appreciates." He enjoys the advantages of wealth, she explains, which, in the eyes of the populace, are valued above any personal merit. Dubious praise indeed, coming from an author who, in the categorization of love, has neatly distinguished between individual worth and ancestral lineage, and who is very adroit in priding herself on the nobility of the heart. On the other hand, the approval of Leone Ebreo is unequivocal. The author's preference for his work and her indebtedness to it are plainly stated. Among those who wrote objectively about the essence of love, rather than subjectively about their own experiences, Varchi declares, Leone Ebreo has dealt with the subject more comprehensively than any other philosopher, with more doctrine and more truth.

Also specific is Aragona's use of Varchi's authority. His doctrine and philosophical training are used to give legitimacy and method to the debate and to validate her arguments. His moral character and his credibility as a philosopher and writer are therefore defended against the attacks of his enemies. At the same time, however, Tullia's poking continuous fun at Varchi's scholarly procedures and scholastic logic has the effect of undermining the reader's confidence in scientifically deduced theories and definitions, which, at times, can be patently absurd and contrary to experience. His competence in matters of love is cut down to size in a discussion of his intellectual and literary merits. He prefers not to indulge in love poetry, and theorizing about love is not his field of endeavor. People say, and he is willing to admit, that he is shy of arguing philosophical points. Above all, contrary to Renaissance dialogues generally, in which the views under discussion are attributed to well-known writers or voiced by characters who represent them, Aragona does not delegate to Varchi the authorship of her theory.[38]

From the beginning, and for a while, the debate unfolds in such a way as to distribute the burden of the demonstration between the two characters, thus giving the impression that theirs is a two-sided, well-argued search for the true nature of love. The presence of two speakers debating all sides of the question camouflages the didactic nature of the dialogue. But there is no dichotomy of opinion, no multiplicity of views from which the reader can choose. And, after Tullia has gathered the reins of the discussion in her hands, it is clear that only one conception of love, namely hers, will be allowed to take shape. And there is no doubt that Tullia's voice is that of the author herself, for the editor's preface has so told the reader.

It is Aragona's literary accomplishment that the characterizations of Tullia and Varchi are not born from a difference in their opinions, as is the case with many contemporary dialogues. These characters are differentiated in their temperament, mental idiosyncrasies, and style of speech. The man is depicted as a stolid pedagogue, whose rigid argumentative procedures and pedantic leanings lead him straight into logical pitfalls. He is kindly, but misogynistic and, at times, patronizing. Outstanding among Tullia's traits is a remarkable ability to discern distant relationships and a knack for deflating philosophical shibboleths in colorful and popular language. She in turns flatters and mocks Varchi, pleads ignorance and shyness, all the while leading him

---

38. On the dialogic strategies and on the many categorizations of the genre, see Virginia Cox, *The Renaissance Dialogue*, which also provides ample bibliography.

straight where she wants him. Her manners are seductive at times, but more often reflective of a commonsensical woman, who appeals to her own understanding and experience of things and refuses to submit blindly to authority. The discussion's banter between the two main characters is so lively and seemingly so true to life that many a literary historian has fallen into the fallacy of viewing the dialogue as the transcription of an actual conversation instead of a dialogue that has taken its personae to be faithful representations of the people they purport to represent.[39]

But Aragona was eminently aware of her work as a literary construct. In her dedication to Cosimo I, she inscribes her dialogue into the illustrious vernacular tradition and offers it as a contribution to the duke's plan to uphold the cultural supremacy of Tuscany against the claims of other Italian regions. Prestigious texts are quoted throughout the debate itself. When Varchi's vexations are compared with those suffered by famous men of the past and by contemporary intellectuals, that literary continuity is made real by the very description of the conversations taking place in Tullia's house. Aragona also adheres to this tradition of refined learning by obeying the rules of literary etiquette. From the editor's preface, for example, the reader learns that the dialogue was published, and the identity of the female character is revealed, only by Muzio's decision, for reasons of fairness and consistency. In the dialogue itself, the debate is ushered in by Tullia with a topos of self-abasement, and it is closed, also by her, with a gracious declaration of modesty. These were laws of literary decorum, to which Tullia refers at the end as "appropriate and decorous fashion."

AFTERMATH

In Tullia d'Aragona's times, the debate on the nature of love held the interest of all educated classes. The term *love* covered a large spectrum of feelings and experiences, from the longing for sensual gratification, to the desire for wealth and honor, to the intellectual pursuit of the divine. In the more popular dialogues on love, the writer's interest focused on human relationships. This special concern attests to a widespread need for understanding one's emotions and for mediating the conflict that existed between the conduct of the individual and the ethical code imposed by religion.

39. Pozzi speaks of "historical truth" in *Trattati d'amore del Cinquecento* (Bari-Rome: Laterza, 1975; reprint of G. Zonta's edition of 1912), p. xxx, and in "Aspetti della trattatistica d'amore" in *Lingua, cultura, società. Saggi sulla letteratura italiana del Cinquecento* (Alessandria: Edizioni dell' Orso, 1989), p. 87. His interpretation is consistent with the notion of the dialogue as a transcription of an actual conversation.

The Christian concept of morality, with its rigid dichotomy of the spiritual and the physical realms, stigmatized any concession to the sensual nature of humankind. Sexual pleasure was considered a sin, sanctioned only by marriage, providing it was immediately connected with procreation. In practice, however, men excusably indulged in it, until the time came presumably to redirect their lives and submit all resources to the requirements of a career, which, more often than not, was being pursued within the ranks of church bureaucracy. Women's destiny and conduct were classified according to categories that reflected the practical and the moral obligations of men. Nuns, wives, and prostitutes were respectively pledged to religious discipline and abstention, to matrimonial duties and to the venal purveyance of sexual pleasure. It is not without significance that an extraordinarily large class of courtesans flourished in the cities, especially in Rome and Venice, where greater possibilities of bureaucratic employment existed for men.

During the Counter Reformation, the church began to impose on its members and on the faithful a code more consonant with its own principles of behavior. Tullia d'Aragona, whose expectations and life-style had been fashioned in an earlier, more permissive society, attempted to resist the tide of restrictive regulations. Not only was her livelihood at risk, but her very sense of self, as a refined purveyor of intellectual and sensual rewards, was seriously threatened. Her defense came in the form of a theory that calls for a radical revision of standard principles, for a morality of love that acknowledges the dichotomous nature of both women and men.

Aragona's dialogue became famous upon publication as the work of a celebrated courtesan and has maintained that fame ever since. Its significance, however, and the complex motivations for writing it, have largely been misunderstood or ignored. I hope that the present study and the translation of the *Dialogue on the Infinity of Love* will correct some of the misunderstandings incurred by many casual readers and that they will introduce Tullia d'Aragona to the appreciative audience she deserves.

Rinaldina Russell

SUGGESTIONS FOR
FURTHER READING

PRIMARY WORKS

Agrippa of Nettesheim, Henry Cornelius (1486–1535). *De nobilitate et praecellentia foeminei sexus, The Nobility and Preeminence of the Female Sex.* Ed. and trans. Albert Rabil, Jr. Chicago: University of Chicago Press, 1996.

Aragona, Tullia d'. "Dialogo della infinità d'amore." In *Trattati d'amore del Cinquecento,* edited by M. Pozzi, pp. 185–248. Rome-Bari, 1980 (reprint of the 1912 G. Zonta's edition).

Alberti, Leon Battista (1404–72). *The Family in Renaissance Florence.* Trans. Renée Neu Watkins. Columbia, SC: University of South Carolina Press, 1969.

Ariosto, Ludovico (1474–1533). *Orlando Furioso.* Trans. Barbara Reynolds. 2 volumes. New York: Penguin, 1975–77.

Astell, Mary (1666–1731). *The First English Feminist: Reflections on Marriage and Other Writings.* Edited and with an Introduction by Bridget Hill. New York: St. Martin's Press, 1986.

Barbaro, Francesco (1390–1454). *On Wifely Duties.* Trans. Benjamin Kohl. In *The Earthly Republic,* edited by B. Kohl and R. G. Witt, pp. 179–228. Philadelphia: University of Pennsylvania Press, 1978. Translation of the Preface and Book 2.

Bembo, Pietro (1470–1547). *Gli Asolani,* edited by Giorgio Dilemmi. Florence: Presso l'Accademia della Crusca, 1991. *Gli Asolani.* Trans. R. B. Gottfried. Bloomington, IN: Indiana University Press, 1954.

Boccaccio, Giovanni (1313–75). *Concerning Famous Women.* Trans. Guido A. Guarino. New Brunswick, NJ: Rutgers University Press, 1963.

———. *Corbaccio or The Labyrinth of Love.* Trans. Anthony K. Cassell. Second revised edition. Binghamton, NY: Medieval and Renaissance Texts and Studies, 1993.

Bruni, Leonardo (1370–1444). "On the Study of Literature (1405) to Lady Battista Malatesta of Montefeltro." In *The Humanism of Leonardo Bruni: Selected Texts.* Trans. and with an Introduction by Gordon Griffiths, James Hankins, and David Thompson, pp. 240–51. Binghamton, NY: Medieval and Renaissance Texts and Studies, 1987.

Castiglione, Baldesar (1478–1529). *The Courtier.* Trans. George Bull. New York: Viking Penguin, 1967.

Elyot, Thomas (1490–1546). *Defence of Good Women: The Feminist Controversy of the Renaissance.* Facsimile Reproductions. Ed. Diane Bornstein. New York: Delmar, 1980.

Erasmus, Desiderius (1467–1536). *The Praise of Folly.* Trans. with an introduction and commentary by Clarence H. Miller. New Haven, CT: Yale University Press, 1979. Best edition, since it indicates additions to the text between 1511 and 1516.

———. *Erasmus on Women.* Ed. Erika Rummel. Toronto: University of Toronto Press, 1996.

Ficino, Marsilio (1433–99). *Commentary on Plato's Symposium.* Ed. and trans. Sears Jayne. Dallas, TX: Spring Publications, 1985.

Kempe, Margery (1373–1439). *The Book of Margery Kempe.* Trans. Barry A. Windeatt. New York: Viking Penguin, 1986.

King, Margaret L., and Albert Rabil, Jr., eds. *Her Immaculate Hand: Selected Works By and About the Women Humanists of Quattrocento Italy.* Binghamton, NY: Medieval and Renaissance Texts and Studies, 1983; 2d revised paperback edition, 1991.

Klein, Joan Larsen, ed. *Daughters, Wives, and Widows: Writings by Men about Women and Marriage in England, 1500–1640.* Urbana, IL: University of Illinois Press, 1992.

Knox, John (1505–1572). *The Political Writings of John Knox: The First Blast of the Trumpet Against the Monstrous Regiment of Women and Other Selected Works.* Ed. Marvin A. Breslow. Washington: Folger Shakespeare Library, 1985.

Kors, Alan C. and Edward Peters, eds. *Witchcraft in Europe, 1100–1700: A Documentary History.* Philadelphia: University of Pennsylvania Press, 1972.

Krämer, Heinrich, and Jacob Sprenger. *Malleus Maleficarum* (ca. 1487). Trans. Montague Summers. London: The Pushkin Press, 1928; reprinted New York: Dover, 1971. The "Hammer of Witches," a convenient source for all the misogynistic commonplaces on the eve of the sixteenth century and an important text in the witch craze of the following centuries.

Leone Ebreo (c. 1435–c. 1560). *Dialoghi d'amore.* Ed. S. Caramella. Bari: Laterza, 1929; translated by F. Friedeberg-Sieley and J. H. Barnes as *The Philosophy of Love.* With an introduction by C. Roth. London: The Socino Press, 1937.

de Lorris, William, and Jean de Meun. *The Romance of the Rose.* Trans. Charles Dahlbert. Princeton: Princeton University Press, 1971; repr. University Press of New England, 1983.

Marguerite d'Angoulême, Queen of Navarre (1492–1549). *The Heptameron.* Trans. P. A. Chilton. New York: Viking Penguin, 1984.

de Pizan, Christine (1365–1431). *The Book of the City of Ladies.* Trans. Earl Jeffrey Richards. Foreword by Marina Warner. New York: Persea Books, 1982.

———. *The Treasure of the City of Ladies.* Trans. Sarah Lawson. New York: Viking Penguin, 1985. Also trans. and with an Introduction by Charity Cannon Willard. Ed. and with an Introduction by Madeleine P. Cosman. New York: Persea Books, 1989.

Spenser, Edmund (1552–1599). *The Faerie Queene.* Ed. Thomas P. Roche, Jr., with the assistance of C. Patrick O'Donnell, Jr. New Haven: Yale University Press, 1978.

Speroni, Sperone. *Dialogo d'amore.* In *Trattatisti del Cinquecento.* Ed. Mario Pozzi, I: 511–63. Milan-Naples: Ricciardi, 1978.

Teresa of Avila, Saint (1515–1582). *The Life of Saint Teresa of Avila by Herself.* Trans. J. M. Cohen. New York: Viking Penguin, 1957.

Vives, Juan Luis (1492–1540). *The Instruction of the Christian Woman.* Trans. Rycharde Hyrde. London, 1524, 1557.

Weyer, Johann (1515–1588). *Witches, Devils and Doctors in the Renaissance: Johann Weyer, De praestigiis daemonum.* Ed. George Mora with Benjamin G. Kohl, Erik Midelfort, and Helen Bacon. Trans. John Shea. Binghamton, NY: Medieval and Renaissance Texts and Studies, 1991.

Wilson, Katharina M., ed. *Medieval Women Writers.* Athens, GA: University of Georgia Press, 1984.

————. *Women Writers of the Renaissance and Reformation.* Athens, GA: University of Georgia Press, 1987.

Wilson, Katharina M., and Frank J. Warnke, eds. *Women Writers of the Seventeenth Century.* Athens, GA: University of Georgia Press, 1989.

Women Writers in English 1350–1850: 30 volumes projected, 8 published through 1995. Oxford University Press.

SECONDARY WORKS

Aurigemma, Marcello. "La teoria dei modelli e i trattati d'amore," in *Lirica, poemi e trattati civili del Cinquecento,* pp. 9–53. Rome-Bari: Laterza, 1973.

Bassanese, Fiora. "Private Lives and Public Lies: Texts by Courtesans of the Italian Renaissance." *Texas Studies in Literature and Languages* 30 (1988): 295–319.

Beilin, Elaine V. *Redeeming Eve: Women Writers of the English Renaissance.* Princeton: Princeton University Press, 1987.

Benson, Pamela Joseph. *The Invention of Renaissance Woman: The Challenge of Female Independence in the Literature and Thought of Italy and England.* University Park, PA: Pennsylvania State University Press, 1992.

Bloch, R. Howard. *Medieval Misogyny and the Invention of Western Romantic Love.* Chicago: University of Chicago Press, 1991.

Bongi, Salvatore. "Rime della Signora Tullia d'Aragona." In *Annali di Gabriel Giolito de' Ferrari,* I:150–99. Rome: Presso i principali librai, 1890.

Burke, Peter. "The Renaissance Dialogue." *Renaissance Studies* 3, no. 1 (1989): 1–12.

Clark, Elizabeth A. *Ascetic Piety and Women's Faith: Essays on Late Ancient Christianity.* Lewiston, NY: Edwin Mellen Press, 1986.

Cohen, Elizabeth S. "'Courtesans' and 'Whores': Words and Behavior in Roman Streets." *Women Studies. Special Issue: Women in the Renaissance: An Interdisciplinary Forum. MLA (1989),* Eds. Ann Rosalind Jones and Betty Travitsky. Vol. 19, no. 1 (1991): 201-208.

Cox, Virginia. *The Renaissance Dialogue.* Cambridge: Cambridge University Press, 1992.

Croce, Benedetto. "Girolamo Muzio." In *Poeti e scrittori del pieno e tardo Rinascimento,* I: 198–210. Bari: Laterza, 1945.

————. "Benedetto Varchi." In *Poeti e scrittori del pieno e tardo Rinascimento*, III: 156–59.

Davis, Natalie Zemon. *Society and Culture in Early Modern France*. Stanford: Stanford University Press, 1975. Especially chapters 3 and 5.

Dionisotti, Carlo. "La letteratura italiana nell'età del Concilio di Trento." In *Geografia e storia della letteratura italiana*, pp. 183–204. Turin: Einaudi, 1967.

Dixon, Suzanne. *The Roman Family*. Baltimore: Johns Hopkins University Press, 1992.

Fahy, Conor. "Three Early Renaissance Treatises on Women." *Italian Studies* 2 (1956): 30–55.

Ferguson, Margaret W., Maureen Quilligan, and Nancy J. Vickers, eds. *Rewriting the Renaissance: The Discourses of Sexual Difference in Early Modern Europe*. Chicago: University of Chicago Press, 1987.

Gardner, Jane F. *Women in Roman Law and Society*. Bloomington, IN: Indiana University Press, 1986.

Herlihy, David. "Did Women Have a Renaissance? A Reconsideration." *Medievalia et Humanistica*, NS 13 (1985): 1–22.

A History of Women in the West

Volume 1: *From Ancient Goddesses to Christian Saints*. Ed. Pauline Schmitt Pantel. Cambridge, MA: Harvard University Press, 1992.

Volume 2: *Silences of the Middle Ages*. Ed. Christiane Klapisch-Zuber. Cambridge: Harvard University Press, 1992.

Volume 3: *Renaissance and Enlightenment Paradoxes*. Ed. Natalie Zemon Davis and Arlette Farge. Cambridge: Harvard University Press, 1993.

Horowitz, Maryanne Cline. "Aristotle and Woman." *Journal of the History of Biology* 9 (1976): 183–213.

Hull, Suzanne W. *Chaste, Silent and Obedient: English Books for Women, 1475–1640*. San Marino, CA: The Huntington Library, 1982.

Jordan, Constance. *Renaissance Feminism: Literary Texts and Political Models*. Ithaca: Cornell University Press, 1990.

Kelly, Joan. "Did Women Have a Renaissance?" In her *Women, History and Theory*. Chicago: University of Chicago Press, 1984. Also in Renate Bridenthal, Claudia Koonz, and Susan M. Stuard, eds. *Becoming Visible: Women in European History*, 2d ed., 175–202. (Boston: Houghton Mifflin, 1987).

————. "Early Feminist Theory and the *Querelle des Femmes*." In *Women, History and Theory*. Chicago: University of Chicago Press, 1984.

Kelso, Ruth. *Doctrine for the Lady of the Renaissance*. Foreword by Katharine M. Rogers. Urbana, IL: University of Illinois Press, 1956, 1978.

King, Margaret L. *Women of the Renaissance*. Foreword by Catharine R. Stimpson. Chicago: University of Chicago Press, 1991.

Kristeller, P. O. *Eight Philosophers of the Italian Renaissance*. Stanford, CA: Stanford University Press, 1964.

————. *Renaissance Thought*. 2 Vols. New York: Harper and Row, 1961.

Laqueur, Thomas. *Making Sex: Body and Gender from the Greeks to Freud.* Cambridge, MA: Harvard University Press, 1990.

Larivaille, Paul. *La vie quotidienne des courtisanes en Italie au temps de la Renaissance.* Paris: Hachette, 1975.

Lerner, Gerda. *The Creation of Feminist Consciousness, 1000–1870.* New York: Oxford University Press, 1994.

———. *The Creation of Patriarchy.* New York: Oxford University Press, 1986.

Lochrie, Karma. *Margery Kempe and Translations of the Flesh.* Philadelphia: University of Pennsylvania Press, 1992.

Maclean, Ian. *The Renaissance Notion of Woman: A Study of the Fortunes of Scholasticism and Medical Science in European Intellectual Life.* Cambridge: Cambridge University Press, 1980.

Maclean, Ian. *Woman Triumphant: Feminism in French Literature, 1610–1652.* Oxford: Clarendon Press, 1977.

Masson, Georgina. "Tullia d'Aragona, the Intellectual Courtesan." In *Courtesans of the Italian Renaissance,* 91–131. London: Secker & Warburg, 1975).

Matter, E. Ann, and John Coakley, eds. *Creative Women in Medieval and Early Modern Italy.* Philadelphia: University of Pennsylvania Press, 1994. (This is a sequel to the Monson collection, listed immediately below.)

Monson, Craig A., ed. *The Crannied Wall: Women, Religion, and the Arts in Early Modern Europe.* Ann Arbor: University of Michigan Press, 1992.

Nelson, John C. *Renaissance Theory of Love.* New York: Columbia University Press, 1958.

Okin, Susan Moller. *Women in Western Political Thought.* Princeton: Princeton University Press, 1979.

Pagels, Elaine. *Adam, Eve and the Serpent.* New York: HarperCollins, 1988.

Pomeroy, Sarah B. *Goddesses, Whores, Wives, and Slaves: Women in Classical Antiquity.* New York: Schocken Books, 1976.

Pozzi, Mario. "Aspetti della trattatistica d'amore." In *Lingua, cultura, società. Saggi sulla letteratura italiana del Cinquecento,* pp. 57–100. Alessandria: Edizioni dell' Orso, 1989.

Robb, Nesca A. *Neoplatonism of the Italian Renaissance.* New York: Octagon Books, 1968.

Rose, Mary Beth, ed. *Women in the Middle Ages and the Renaissance: Literary and Historical Perspectives.* Syracuse: Syracuse University Press, 1986.

Russell, Rinaldina. "Tullia d'Aragona." In *Italian Women Writers,* ed. Rinaldina Russell, 26–34. Westport, CT, and London: Greenwood, 1994.

Snyder, Jon R. *Writing the Scene of Speaking: Theories of Dialogue in the Late Renaissance.* Stanford, CA: Stanford University Press: 1989.

Sommerville, Margaret R. *Sex and Subjectivity: Attitudes to Women in Early-Modern Society.* London: Arnold, 1995.

Stuard, Susan M., "The Dominion of Gender: Women's Fortunes in the High Middle Ages." In Renate Bridental, Claudia Koonz, and Susan M. Stuard, eds., *Becoming Visible: Women in European History,* 2d ed., pp. 153–72. Boston: Houghton Mifflin, 1987.

Tetel, Marcel. *Marguerite de Navarre's Heptameron: Themes, Language and Structure.* Durham, NC: Duke University Press, 1973.

Treggiari, Susan. *Roman Marriage: Iusti Coniuges From the Time of Cicero to the Time of Ulpian.* Oxford: Oxford University Press, 1991.

Walsh. William T. *St. Teresa of Avila: A Biography.* Rockford, IL: TAN Books & Publications, 1987.

Warner, Marina. *Alone of All Her Sex: The Myth and the Cult of the Virgin Mary.* New York: Knopf, 1976.

Wiesner, Merry E. *Women and Gender in Early Modern Europe.* Cambridge: Cambridge University Press, 1987.

Willard, Charity Cannon. *Christine de Pizan: Her Life and Works.* New York: Persea Books, 1984.

Wilson, Katharina, ed. *An Encyclopedia of Continental Women Writers.* New York: Garland, 1991.

DIALOGUE ON
THE INFINITY OF LOVE

To the Most excellent
Signora Tullia d'Aragona
from Muzio Iustinapolitano

My valiant lady, as a human being is composed of two parts, one of them earthly and mortal, the other celestial and eternal, so too there are two types of beauty, as you know full well. These two types of beauty, each following the essence of its respective part, are frail and ephemeral in the one case, vigorous and immortal in the other. Now these two remarkable beacons of our body and soul present themselves to other people by way of the senses and arouse in their emotions and in their souls that desire which is called love. Once again, there are two kinds of love, precisely as there are two types of beauty, because, as some people are enamored of sheer physical loveliness while others are illuminated by the light that shines inside, each individual is drawn to that object that appears to him to be most desirable.

Just as we have said that the two types of beauty correspond to the essence of those different parts which they respectively ornament, it follows that the effects of the two kinds of love differ as well. This is because when the flower of our earthly garb begins to fade with the passing of time, it is equally certain that desire for this flower is bound to wilt. On the other hand, since the true light burns brighter in our souls with every day that passes by, it is understandable that once a person feels that he has been irradiated by that light, then he will be more greatly inflamed by it from one day to the next.

Since these matters are not perhaps understood by everyone, there have been some people who were amazed that, at the very age when they imagine one ought to have put an end to the pangs of love, I still manifest no less a love for you than I used to all those years ago. And in their minds, they have perhaps condemned me for this and have lowered their esteem for me. I wish to testify openly to them that not only do I love you just as much as in the past, but actually now love you far more than then, in proportion to the increase, in you, of that beauty which originally induced me to fall in love with you and because of my continuing cognition of that beauty. And if perhaps those critics do not perceive that beauty of yours, it is because they do not gaze upon you with the same eyes that I do. For if they turned to contemplate you with a vision similar to my own, they would fix their sight in a direction that would cause them to be irradiated with love for you and to praise me for my continuing love.

Great proof to me of the increase in your beauty is given by this dialogue which you have written, *On the Infinity of Love*. Now, in writing to you, I shall de- 51 sist from trying to praise it adequately for, indeed, I can hardly see a greater way of showering praise on it than by having judged that the time has come to remove it from its burial in the darkness. In your typically courteous manner, you made me a recipient of your dialogue, as though it were something you wished to share with me and not because it might be something for publication. I, for my part (considering that since my love for you makes me as zealous in seeking honor for you as for myself), could not restrain myself from bringing your work to light. Perhaps there was a very strong element of desire for my own honor in doing this, because it is generally understood that I adore any beauty capable of generating such a glorious offspring, and therefore in the eyes of the most refined spirits I am bound to be honored and praised a good deal for my exploit.

Great, indeed, are the consolations that Love offers to those who truly love. Not only have I taken the liberty of publishing this work of yours without your knowledge, but I have ventured even further. You present a disputation that took place between yourself, Varchi, and Doctor Benucci.[1] Since the dialogue contains many details extolling your praises and virtues, you deemed it unsuitable to refer to yourself by your real name, so out of modesty you chose to pass yourself off as Sabina. I, however, considered it wrong that a dialogue should have one fictitious name amongst two real ones, and I judged that either all the names should be fictitious or all of them real. I realized that if I left yours in its altered form and also altered the other two names, I would have done wrong to those most noble spirits whom it had pleased you to bring to life in your pages. That is why I adopted the plan of leaving those names just as they were and restoring "Tullia" in place of "Sabina." I would have done this for no other reason, indeed, than because of your choosing to have the no less learned than eloquent Varchi make such honorable mention of me as a person belonging to you, and I know that I have never belonged to any Sabina. I know perfectly well that I have only ever belonged, and still belong, to Signora Tullia. I am sure that what I am saying here would be repeated by the excellent Signor Sperone, if he heard himself referred to as yours in the same way. This much alone, then, I have had the temerity to alter in the dialogue, and my correction has ventured no further.

---

1. For Varchi, see Introduction, p. 25. Lattanzio Benucci was a medical doctor and a frequent guest of Aragona in Florence who exchanged complimentary sonnets with her (Aragona, *Rime*, pp. 51, 123–25). His visit to Tullia's country villa in the summer of 1546 is mentioned in her letter to Varchi dated 25 August. Later in life, Benucci wrote a *Dialogo della lontananza* (1563), in which a Neapolitan lady and the poet Bernardo Cappello converse on the "question" of whether passion is stronger when the lovers are separated or when they are together (M. Pozzi, *Lingua, cultura, società*, p. 87).

For this boldness of mine, and for having your work published, I am assured by Love that you will forgive me, since none other than Love was my instigator. You really should be delighted by this publication, even though it is effected without your consent. If by chance this dialogue were not such as to deserve total praise, you would not be at fault because you intended to keep it hidden, while I solely would be to blame for I chose to issue it. However I am sure that, to your undying reputation, the world will be eternally grateful to me for the fruit of your labors.

To the Most Illustrious Lord
Cosimo de' Medici,
Duke of Florence
—her deeply revered master—
from Tullia d'Aragona

I have for a long while been undecided, most gracious and noble Lord, as to whether I should dedicate to your esteemed Highness a certain discussion, which took place in my home some months ago, on the infinity of love and on some other related questions which were no less attractive, if my judgment is not faulty, than they were difficult to solve. From one point of view, I was intimidated both by the elevated status of Your Lordship and my own lowly condition. I could hardly be certain that I was not distracting You from the multitude of matters of state that beset Your Lordship daily in ensuring the safety and serenity of Your prosperous domain and also in governing and dispensing justice to Your fortunate subjects. On the other hand, I was comforted and even encouraged in my enterprise by the certainty that Your Highness takes deep joy in all literary compositions, especially those which are written in the vernacular tongue so favorably viewed and promoted by Your Illustrious Self, and which deal with subjects either useful or entertaining.[2] I was also driven by a keen desire of my own to show a small token of the affection and devotion I have always felt for Your illustrious and blessed house and to give You special thanks for the favors I have received. Hence, when at last I felt certain that Your Excellency was more likely to turn the infinite courtesy and generosity of his attention to the altitude of the subject in these humble literary labors of mine rather than to the scantness of my gift, I decided to accept the more likely risk of being considered presumptuous by many other people rather than ungrateful by Your Lordship alone. Consequently, and in all humility, I kiss Your sovereign hands and pray God that He may grant You long health and felicity.

2. See Introduction, p. 41.

DIALOGUE ON
THE INFINITY OF LOVE

Speakers: Tullia, Benedetto Varchi, and Signor Lattanzio Benucci

TULLIA: No one could have dropped by at a better moment, my dear and excellent Signor Benedetto, nor could we have wished to see anyone so congenial and so eagerly anticipated!

VARCHI: I am indeed pleased to hear that, my dear and most esteemed Signora Tullia. All the more because I was afraid that maybe I had, if not totally ruined, at least disturbed your conversation, which—I am certain—can only have been delightful and must have concerned elevated matters, worthy of the people here and of this place, where the subjects under discussion are always no less useful and important than they are lively and entertaining. So I was already sorry I had turned up, and I said to myself: Woe is me, love takes me whither I wouldst not go, for I was afraid not so much of being presumptuous as of annoying the very person I most desired to please. But if I have not caused you any annoyance, I am happy indeed, as well as grateful for your graciousness and for the good will of these kind sirs and gentlemen in your company, with whose permission I'll take a seat. On one condition, however: that you carry on the discussions on which you had embarked, unless, perhaps, they are such that you deem me unworthy to join in.[3]

TULLIA: On the contrary, that was one of the many reasons why we wanted you here with us. Yet I rather wonder whether you may not end up feeling a little uncomfortable and perhaps regretting the fact that you came over, particularly because it was my turn to speak, and for the reasons that you will shortly hear: not only am I a woman—and you have some complex philosophical reasons for considering women less meritorious and intrinsically less

---

3. The subject of the previous conversation will be stated by Benucci at the end of the debate on the infinity of love, p. 104.

perfect than men—but what is more, I do not possess either sufficient learning or verbal ornaments, as you are well aware.[4]

VARCHI: I can hardly believe, my dear Signora Tullia, that you can consider me as uncouth as Cimone.[5] I am not a fellow so inexpert in worldly matters and the facts of nature as not to know, at least in part, how great the power of women over men is, was, and always shall be, thanks to their spiritual qualities and, even more, to the beauty of their bodies. I would know as much had I not seen or heard any other woman but you! But we'll have plenty of time to discuss this matter on another occasion. Let me now say that you are doing a grievous wrong to the great affection that I feel for you and to my powers of judgment. (Indeed, it may well be that my judgment is below average in all other matters, but on the question of assessing your qualities, and revering and cultivating them, it is simply supreme.) You are also doing a disservice to your in-born nobility and goodness if you let yourself imagine that when I am in your company, gazing on your appearance or listening to your words, I experience any other sensation than deep pleasure, ineffable sweetness, and unequaled contentment. Would I then be so ignorant, so mean and ungrateful that I could ignore or pass by without praising that beauty, virtue, and refinement of yours, which is bound to be honored, admired, and adored by anyone who has either seen it for himself or heard tell of it from others? I don't want to set myself up in any way as the equal of our very learned, refined and gracious Signor Sperone, nor hold myself on a par with the exalted accomplishments of our dear Signor Muzio.[6] Far from it: I wish to offer them the deference which is their due, and which in every way I owe them, unless it be in the matter of appreciating your own worth, my dear Tullia, the praises of which I have perhaps not been able to sing to their exalted tune. Sperone, in his prose, and Muzio, both in his ornate prose and in different poetic meters, have written so much, and in such style, about you, that their texts "will last as long as the universe is in motion."[7] In fact, I believe I surpass them in this one respect as much as they rise above me in wit and eloquence. Finally, let me say that if I might be permitted a single complaint about one to whom I owe unreserved praise, I could venture to prove how unjust was your accusation of a moment ago.

4. Varchi had expressed his views on women in his lectures "Dichiarazione sopra il venticinquesimo canto del *Purgatorio* di Dante" and "Lezione nella quale si ragiona della natura," delivered in the Florentine Academy in 1543 and 1547 respectively (*Opere*, 2:289a, 655, 657b–658a).

5. Cimone, a youth bred in the forest by wild animals, is the protagonist of Boccaccio's *Decameron* 5.1.

6. For Sperone Speroni, Muzio Giustinapolitano, and their writings in praise of Aragona, see the Introduction, pp. 23–24, 36.

7. This is a translation of Dante's line: "Che dureran quanto 'l moto lontano" (*Inferno* 1.60).

TULLIA: It will never be my intention to slight those whose merits accord them the greatest honors, and among them your good self. Now if, my dear learned Varchi, I mentioned that I wondered whether you might feel uncomfortable, it was not because of any belief on my part that you were lukewarm in affection toward me. For I know only too well that your love is on a greater scale than I can deserve. Furthermore, I understand how your natural disposition is to give precedence to the wishes of others over your own inclinations. You make a practice of never denying things to other people and prefer to cultivate what pleases them rather than what suits yourself. Also, you constantly engage in attractive and praiseworthy lines of study while staying abreast of a thousand domestic cares and attending to the countless vexations brought about partly by those who know your virtues and love them and partly by those who know them well but love them not. This endurance of yours is certainly great.[8] However, it is not a point I want to dwell on, as I don't wish to give the impression that I'm paying back the rich and copious praise which you addressed to me. I will not say that you showed lack of discernment in so praising me, but rather too much zeal in your love for me (since flattery would be quite alien to you), and each item of praise was as unsuited to me as it was fitting for yourself, whose goodness and virtue. . . . Yet we must not use up time on marginal matters, especially in your presence and you being always the one who makes light of himself and ennobles the reputation of others. So I'm pleading with you to be so kind as to solve a question which a short while back was proposed for discussion. At a certain point we diverged from that topic, after we had agreed to await your arrival and ask you to set the terms of the question for us. After that we got into other diversions. And take good care not to turn down this request, or else we might not think you the fellow you pretend to be and the person we know that you really are.

VARCHI: I can hardly tell who or what I want to be taken for, except that I wish to make sure to be known as your good friend and devoted servant. If I

8. The preeminent position quickly acquired by Varchi in the Florentine literary world made him the object of disparaging gossip both regarding his learning and his private morality. What purportedly were slanderous accusations of rape of a minor brought about his arrest in 1545. His release was obtained by the duke after he pleaded guilty. His amorous pursuits of young male pupils caused him considerable embarrassment before and after his friendship with Aragona. Varchi attributed such mishaps to the jealousy and envy of his competitors and complained about it in "Lesson on Envy" (*Opere,* 2:582–850). What might have also caused the resentment of many against him was his tendency to get embroiled with other literati over linguistic minutiae and to offend those humanists who maintained the superiority of Latin over the vernacular (cf. "Vita di Benedetto Varchi," in *Lezioni sul Dante e prose varie* [Florence, 1841], 1:xxiv, xliii; Umberto Pirotti, *Benedetto Varchi e la cultura del suo tempo* [Florence: Olschki, 1971], pp. 14–15, 28–29). Cf. footnote 81.

really thought I could satisfy you even to a trifling extent, though I merely dropped by here today to listen and learn, rather than to speak, I would not mind at all, rather I would be very pleased. . . .

TULLIA: Please do not enter into a set of excuses that are much too banal for a man of your distinction. Why not preserve your modesty for another occasion and for people who do not know you? Otherwise I shall conclude that you think you've been given too little praise and are waiting for some more.

VARCHI: I can easily forgive your last remark, as well as the charmingly untruthful things you said about me, when I reflect that it was all a display of your eloquence and an unnecessary display at that. Yet I must forgive you for it, as I said, since I am unable and unwilling to disobey you in whatever matter where I may be of avail to you. So you shall be obliged to make penance for your misdeed. For when these gentlemen in our company hear me speak, they will form the view that you have shown scant judgment and excessive flattery.

TULLIA: Don't you worry about that. Leave me with the problem and come back to a clarification of the question we proposed just now.

VARCHI: What question are you talking about? First tell me and then I can try to satisfy you, if I am able to. On one condition, though: that afterwards you fill me in on the discussions which you said you had commenced a little while before I arrived here. Because I noticed that you were all full of concentration and greatly enjoying yourselves.

TULLIA: I'm overjoyed, for if I'm not accustomed to denying something legitimate to most people, to you I can scarcely make or devise a refusal. The question proposed for discussion is as follows: "Is it possible to love within limits?" Can't you give an answer to this?

VARCHI: I wish I hadn't promised in the first place.

TULLIA: Why so?

VARCHI: I don't understand the terms of the proposition, so how can I possibly solve the question?

TULLIA: I know the tricks you are up to. Please do me a favor, if you have the slightest affection for me, and leave your excuses and witticisms to one side. If I can scarcely see the light, that's no reason for you to bandage my eyes completely.

VARCHI: What a splendid way women have! They reinterpret everything after their own fashion. Whoever they deal with, at whatever place or time, the uppermost thing in their minds is to come out the victors. However, since the one with the power around here wants it to be this way, let's make a virtue out of necessity, considering that it is and so will have to be the case. Moreover, I am more than delighted by it, since your entreaty was so framed as to raise all my spirits to a new vigor.

TULLIA: What are you saying now? A whole lot of spirits are in the air, are they? And they're molesting you? I thought that entreaties would exorcise them rather than attract them to a person!

VARCHI: And you say I go in for witticism! All right, let's dismiss the spirits to anyone who wants them and people possessed by spirits to anyone who can bear them. And now tell me: how would you answer if someone were to ask you whether the words "limit" and "end" mean the same thing?

TULLIA: Now I'm the one who can't follow you.

VARCHI: I wonder if these gentlemen won't start laughing at the way we're carrying on: we come from the same town but we can't understand each other, as the saying goes. What I was asking is whether the limit to a given phenomenon can be called its end.

TULLIA: Please just give me an example, if it's not too much trouble.

VARCHI: When a person has arrived at the "limit" of some given object, can it be said that he has reached its "end"?

TULLIA: I'd like that to be made a little clearer.

VARCHI: When a surveyor, as he measures a field or any other area, has reached its furthest limit, in such a way that there is no part of it left over to measure, would you say that he has reached the "end" of it?

TULLIA: Yes, I would say so. To me, phrases like "the final," "ultimate," "limit" and "end," of whatever it may be, seem to have the same meaning.

VARCHI: That's well answered. It means, therefore, that the things that lack an end will also be without a limit and, inversely, those that have no limit will also be lacking an end.

TULLIA: What are you aiming at now? I wouldn't want you to be tying me up inside this plethora of "ends" and "limits."

VARCHI: You seem unnaturally suspicious today and far more so than is your normal manner. Yet you must be aware that once you have conceded the evident truth, namely, that "end" and "limit" stand for the same thing, you can hardly deny what necessarily follows, which is that one who has no end, also has no limit—and the clauses can be reversed, of course. What are you worried about? What makes you so hesitant to concede something you know cannot be denied?

TULLIA: I'm afraid I might be embroiled in God knows what. There's one thing I can't get over, and that's the way these logicians fog up the other person's mind at their first opportunity. They start pronouncing affirmatives and negatives; they want you to say "yes" and "no" at their prompting; they hardly lay off until their side of the argument gets the upper hand, whether rightly or wrongly. Things come to such a head that I usually compare them with the Gypsies when they carry on with their tricks.

VARCHI: You could not have chosen a better argument to prove to me that I'm not one of those logicians, for the very reason that logical discourse does the precise opposite of what you imagine.

TULLIA: Ha! You shan't catch me out like that. I don't mean the proper brand of logic, but the bogus sophistry which is all the modern vogue.

VARCHI: Let's not get into whether it's modern or not: please answer me one thing. Are you ready to concede in words what you've already admitted to me in effect?

TULLIA: Yes I am, but what will flow from it?

VARCHI: Quite simply that if I can prove to you that love has no end, then your query will be resolved.

TULLIA: Just slow down a second: you're very speedy at resolving a problem! For my part, I believe there are a number of tricky steps still ahead of us. And I can't see my way clear to accepting this conclusion of yours. I would really prefer to have it clarified at greater length by you, and at a relaxed pace, since, in any case, time is not pressing. None of the people around us has a more important engagement they should be going on to, or something they would prefer to do than to hear this out.

VARCHI: I'm sure that you have everything at your fingertips and speak this way just to make me say more. And that is all right. But now tell me: are "love" and "to love" not one and the same thing?

TULLIA: Do you really mean what you've just said?

VARCHI: I most certainly do.

TULLIA: Come on, stop talking nonsense. There am I, asking you to speak more plainly and you start going in for riddles and try to raise a laugh from us. Honestly, I never realized you were such a prankster, and I could use an even ruder term for you!

VARCHI: It is you who makes me laugh! Do drop the prattle and try to answer the question I am putting to you.

TULLIA: And what exactly is that?

VARCHI: Whether "love" and "to love" are the same thing.

TULLIA: In faith, Sir, no, they are not. There, you did want me to give clear questions a clear answer.

VARCHI: I suppose you'd hardly answer difficult questions, if your heart isn't up to answering the easy ones! Anyway, if "love" and "to love" are not the same, then they must obviously be different from each other.

TULLIA: Yes, Sir. This is a brand of logic that I too can understand, and if all logical deductions were formed like your last proposition, I could answer them all in an instant.

VARCHI: It is not enough to say "Yes, Sir" like that.

TULLIA: What then, must I prove it to you?

VARCHI: Certainly I want you to prove it for me.

TULLIA: Even if I were unable or unfit to prove it, I still would not accept that "love" and "to love" are identical, because I have heard and been convinced countless times that it is impossible to prove things that are clear and obvious in themselves.[9]

VARCHI: That is very true; you have heard and been convinced of the right thing. However, ours is not one of those cases.

TULLIA: Then why don't you prove the opposite of my assertion?

VARCHI: You'd be in trouble if this were a judicial hearing, because our esteemed jurists would not allow it.[10] So are you sure you don't want to come up with a couple of differences between them?

TULLIA: I could find a thousand.

VARCHI: Name one, then.

TULLIA: What shall I say? What about this: "love" is a noun and "to love" is a verb.

VARCHI: You couldn't have answered better. Indeed, that is the sole difference that exists between them.

TULLIA: That's all I need in order to prove that they are not the same, because if a thousand points of similarity are not sufficient to make one thing identical to another, a single dissimilarity suffices to make it different.

VARCHI: Very well said! But what difference do you believe there is between a noun and a verb?

TULLIA: That's something you'd have to ask a schoolmaster, because I have no particular competence in grammar.

VARCHI: It would be a fine thing for students if their teachers were so knowledgeable. It's not one of their duties to know this, in fact. What is more, I'm not putting the question to you as a grammarian, so don't make such a fuss out of giving me the answer to it.

TULLIA: What if I say that verbs imply time, whereas nouns connote meaning without time?

VARCHI: Now I can tell that you are learned in every way and pretend to know nothing just to force me to do the talking. But if the only difference between "love" and "to love" is the one you mentioned, what the philosophers

9. That is, axioms cannot be proved. See Varchi, "Lezione nella quale si ragiona della natura," *Opere*, 2:649b. Ultimately the concept of axiom goes back to Aristotle, *Prior and Posterior Analitics* 16a13, 72a17, 75a41, 76b14.

10. That is, in judicial cases, a contention cannot be sustained by disproving the opposite. For Varchi's judicial training, see Pirotti, *Varchi*, pp. 5, 7–9.

call an "accident," rather than a "substance," why won't you concede right away that "love" and "to love" stand for the same thing?

TULLIA: Because it seemed very odd to me that such a limited notion as a noun should have the same status as the extended reference of a verb.

VARCHI: I refuse to rebut every point, because I know that you're provoking me. Do you really think I don't know that you are as aware as I am that nouns have priority in a clause and therefore enjoy greater status than verbs?

TULLIA: Where on earth could I have learned such a thing? From which author? From the writer who likes to compose grammatical polemics?

VARCHI: Where indeed? From which authority could you have learned the opposite?

TULLIA: From no one. And I'll admit to you that until now I never thought about which of the two is to be considered more or less perfect than the other. Right now I'm convinced that neither enjoys greater status than the other.

VARCHI: And where did you pick up that notion?

TULLIA: From you, Sir. I can't deny it and I wouldn't want to.

VARCHI: You couldn't have got it from me.

TULLIA: Why not?

VARCHI: Because nouns are the more noble of the two.

TULLIA: See how quickly you fall into self-contradiction!

VARCHI: In which respect?

TULLIA: If nouns are nobler than verbs, then it follows that they can't be the same thing, as you stated a moment ago was the case with "love" and "to love." See how your logic doesn't always work out!

VARCHI: You're being too hasty in correcting me and blaming logic, which deserves to be venerated by one who is dedicated to inquiring after the truth, as I am certain that you are.

TULLIA: Please find the truth in this paradox, and instruct me as to how two things can be one and the same when they differ in degree of merit from each other, and then I'll venerate the logical method.

VARCHI: You certainly should bring yourself to do so, because even though something, considered in itself, simply, and in one respect, cannot differ from itself, or be more or less noble than it already is, when it is viewed in relation to something else and from different viewpoints, it may well be the way I said it is.[11] There is no question about it.

---

11. Here Varchi distinguishes between the Aristotelian concepts of essence and accident. The first pertains to the quality essential to the nature of a thing and is not predicated of anything else; the second refers to the qualities that may or may not be possessed by a thing and can be asserted or denied of it (*Metaphysics* 4.30.1025a30–32).

TULLIA: I believe what you are saying, but I don't quite understand it.

VARCHI: We must trust reason, not authority. What I'm saying is that if you consider the same thing from different angles and relate it to a whole range of other objects, it can turn out to be more or less worthy than itself and, consequently, other than itself.

TULLIA: I'd like to see an example of this.

VARCHI: Is it not the case that God loves Himself?

TULLIA: Yes, that is so.

VARCHI: Therefore He is both the lover and the beloved?

TULLIA: He is.

VARCHI: And which of the two do you consider the nobler, the lover or the beloved?[12]

TULLIA: Without doubt, it is the one who is loved.

VARCHI: Why?

TULLIA: Because the loved one constitutes not just the efficient and formal cause of an act, but also the final one. And the final cause is the most noble of all causes. It leaves the role of material cause to the lover, and this is the least worthy form of causation.

VARCHI: That's an excellent and very erudite response. Hence it follows that God, if considered as the recipient of love, is more noble than Himself when considered as the agent of love.

TULLIA: Yes.

VARCHI: So it turns out that one single thing can be different from itself if considered in the light of different actualizations?

TULLIA: Yes, but what is that supposed to prove?

VARCHI: Only that what seemed totally impossible and totally false a moment ago now turns out to be true and easy to grasp, as the example I just gave you shows.

TULLIA: Yes, but I'll tell you something that's very true: when one is speaking of our mortal world, it's really not acceptable to introduce elements of the divine, because the latter is so perfect that we shall never be able to comprehend it, and each individual is entitled to pronounce his own opinion about it.

---

12. The question of the comparative value of the lover and the beloved went back to Phaedrus' speech in *Symposium*, 179b, and became a favorite topic of *questioni d'amore*. In maintaining the superiority of the lover, Aragona may well have derived concepts, terminology, and dialogic development from Leone's work (*Dialoghi d'amore* [Bari: Laterza, 1929], pp. 57, 203–213, 229, 536–37). Varchi's discussion of the same topic in "Sopra alcune quistioni d'amore. Quistione prima: Qual sia più nobile, o l'amante o l'amato," can be traced to the same source and cannot be considered a proof of Varchi's preponderant role in the authorship of Aragona's dialogue, as some have argued.

VARCHI: You're right to view the gulf between mortal and immortal world as too great to leap across, for there is no comparison, no scale of proportions to link them. We shall never be capable of comprehending more about God than that His perfection puts Him beyond our very comprehension. Not one of us is sufficient to worship God in a way befitting our own debt to Him, let alone His goodness to us.[13] Perhaps the real point is that in discussing love we were already touching on matters divine, despite what you seem to believe.

TULLIA: I realize that. I didn't imply the contrary. You know perfectly well what I mean. Give me some examples that are easy to follow.

VARCHI: All right, then: which do you think is the worthier thing, to be a father or to be a son?

TULLIA: To be a father. But I beseech you in God's name, let's not get into the subject of the Trinity.

VARCHI: Don't worry about that! Now if you took someone who had both father and sons—and there are plenty such—would he be more deserving than his own self as a father, or as a son?

TULLIA: Clearly as a father, that's incontrovertible. However I can't see that these considerations, true as they may be, help to resolve our doubt.

VARCHI: You will see it soon enough. I'm saying that verbs and nouns considered merely for what they are, in their essence, as the philosophers say, are in effect one and the same thing. Hence the former are no more noble than the latter, and vice versa. But if we look at verbs in a time perspective, as you did yourself a moment ago, and consider them in respect to whether they refer to activity or passivity, which cannot be without that substance—or assistance—that is provided by the nouns, then I maintain that verbs are less perfect. Now have you grasped my point?

TULLIA: I think I can understand, but that doesn't mean I've been convinced. On the contrary, a while back I felt quite certain after the examples that you gave about God and about a person who had father and sons at the same time. But now your last step leaves me quite perplexed, because at the moment when I seem to grasp it, I know it has eluded me. So please furnish further examples, if you want me to get a grip on the argument. And let this justify me, if I have been irritating or importunate in our exchanges.

13. The Neoplatonic notion that God cannot be understood by the human mind (*Enneads* III) is the basic principle of Christian negative theology, as well as a theme of medieval speculative Kabbalah. Aragona may again be paraphrasing Leone Ebreo: "Being infinite and in all respects perfect, [God] cannot be comprehended by the human mind, which is imperfect and limited" (*Dialoghi*, p. 34). In a lecture on *Purgatorio* 17, delivered in the Florentine Academy in August of 1564, Varchi said: "God is pure being, whose infinite perfection cannot be understood by any human intellect" (*Opere*, 2:324a). All translations from Leone Ebreo's work and from other Italian texts are mine.

VARCHI: How could you possibly importune me? Please don't be reluctant to ply me with questions, just as I won't mind answering them. My only regret is that I can't settle your queries as expeditiously as perhaps could be done by one of those schoolmasters that you were telling me to appeal to a short while ago. Anyway, please tell me: which do you hold to be the most perfect, form alone without matter, or form united to matter?[14]

TULLIA: I can't quite understand that.

VARCHI: Which one do you judge to be more worthy, the soul taken by itself, without the body, or the soul and the body together?

TULLIA: Now I can understand. Yet this seems to me to be one of those problems which is actually unproblematic.

VARCHI: Perhaps you can't understand me after all.

TULLIA: Why so?

VARCHI: First give me your answer, and then I'll explain it to you.

TULLIA: Is anyone ignorant of the fact that the whole, body and soul taken together, is more noble and more perfect than the soul by itself?

VARCHI: Well, you, for one, seem to be in the dark about that.

TULLIA: Why?

VARCHI: Because the soul by itself is more perfect and nobler.

TULLIA: That seems to me quite implausible, as well as downright impossible. You yourself would have to admit that at least the two are on a par, because the soul will exert the same power united with the body as it would by itself, being the same identical soul. Even if the body adds nothing to the soul, it still doesn't have to reduce it to any degree.

VARCHI: That's an admission I can't make. The reason is as follows: even if the soul remains identical, it is still more worthy in itself and more noble without the corporeal element than if it were united with the body, in just the same way as a lump of gold has greater purity taken by itself than if it is soiled by mud or mixed in an alloy with lead.[15] At least it is the cause of the compound product, if nothing else. However, we've branched off on too many tangents. Perhaps we're annoying these other gentlemen, who have listened in silence up to this point and may now want us to stop.

TULLIA: Don't you worry about that. Just carry on as you were, and, if possible, smooth things out and unfold them in minute detail, without taking

14. For the concept of matter and form, see *Metaphysics* 7.1013 5; *Physics* 2.193a9–b21. Varchi expounds on the same concepts in "Dell'amore. Lezione una" on *Purgatorio* 17 (1564), now in *Opere*, 2:324b–325a.
15. In his lecture of December 1543 on the creation of the rational soul, Varchi stated, drawing from Aristotle's *De anima* II, that form alone is true being. Matter is so imperfect as to add nothing to form, while form has the same perfection as the whole, but in a more perfect way (*Opere*, 2:318a–318b).

into account what I might or might not know. To tell you the truth, I don't seem to know anything, except that I know nothing.

VARCHI: That itself would be no mean feat. You could compare yourself to Socrates, who was the wisest and most virtuous man in the whole of Greece.

TULLIA: I didn't mean that mine was the Socratic ignorance. You are putting excessively subtle interpretations on what I say. However, if Socrates was so wise and virtuous, why don't you make a practice of imitating him? For as you know, he discussed everything with his friend Diotima and learned all manner of wonderful things from her, especially concerning the mysteries of love.

VARCHI: And what do you think I'm doing?

TULLIA: Quite the opposite of everything that Socrates did. Since he adopted a learning stance, whereas you're imparting lessons.

VARCHI: No, you've got it wrong. Where do you think I derive my modest utterances, if not . . .

TULLIA: Come, come. Tone things down. Go back to the main subject and prove to us in a simpler fashion, if that is possible, that "to love" and "love" are the same thing.

VARCHI: Surely "to love" is an effect of "love"?

TULLIA: Previously I believed that this was so.

VARCHI: Why don't you believe it any more?

TULLIA: Because of love for you.

VARCHI: What? For love of me?

TULLIA: Just that, out of consideration for you.

VARCHI: Oh that would be a fine thing, if consideration for me could cause you to forget the truth.

TULLIA: That's not exactly my point. What I meant is that I can't believe in it anymore because a moment ago you asserted that it was not the case.

VARCHI: But I never said that. Please don't take me for a Calandrino.[16]

TULLIA: Instead, you should admit "I can't remember saying so" or "I didn't mean to say so," since in point of fact you did say it.

VARCHI: Well, I'm just lucky, for there are witnesses who will confirm what I did or did not say.

TULLIA: I don't really want any witness or adjudicator other than yourself.

VARCHI: Rest assured that I wouldn't refuse to admit that I made any statement to you, provided I could remember it. But this time I'm certain I didn't state it.

TULLIA: And if I can show that you did say it, will you then believe me?

---

16. Protagonist of two celebrated stories by Boccaccio, Calandrino is a gullible Florentine painter on whom his fellow artists enjoy playing tricks (*Decameron* 8.3 and 9.3).

VARCHI: No, I won't believe it, not at all.

TULLIA: What if I make you produce the very same statement yourself, and show it to you so obviously, then what would you say?

VARCHI: I'd say that you manage to achieve with words what jugglers can do with their trinkets.

TULLIA: Hold fast, there. Didn't you state that "love" and "to love" are in effect and essence one and the same thing? You can't put up much of a denial about that.

VARCHI: I shall not deny it at all. I reaffirm it emphatically.

TULLIA: And don't you say that "to love" is the effect of "love"?

VARCHI: Yes, I do.

TULLIA: Don't you see what all this leads to? You'd need more than logic to get out of this quandary.

VARCHI: It leads to a lot, and regrettably so. Why are you so amazed and make such a commotion?

TULLIA: Because I'd never come across the notion that cause and effect, that is to say, father and son, were one and the same thing.[17]

VARCHI: Nor had I heard it, except from lawyers.

TULLIA: We're getting down to some real games-playing here. Surely you said a while back that "love" and "to love" are the same, since "to love" is the effect of "love." Isn't that so?

VARCHI: Yes, Madam, and I say it again.

TULLIA: How can this be the case?

VARCHI: Very simply, both for you, after your erudite doubts, and for me, after expressing the truth of the matter.

TULLIA: Wait and see, I'll be the Calandrino around here, not you. How can that be true?

VARCHI: That illusion, that very equivocation which obscured things for you before is dazzling you now. The truth is that if we consider "love" and "to love" both in their essence and as substances, then they come to be the same thing, as we said a moment ago. Yet, if we consider each one of them within the determination of time, then they appear to be different. This impression does not proceed from any real difference in their essence, but from a difference in our way of looking at them. So if you knew that "human being" and "humanity" are the same thing, but can be taken in two different meanings, you would not then be particularly surprised.

TULLIA: I knew you would try to pull one on me! But how can you expect me to believe that a cause and an effect are the same thing?

---

17. The *loci* for the concepts of cause and effect are *Metaphysics* 1.983a and *Physics* 1.184a10; 2.195a.

VARCHI: That's not what I'm driving at. Something that is not the case cannot be taken as such, nor must it be believed to be so.

TULLIA: So, was I in the right?

VARCHI: No, Madam, you were not.

TULLIA: Come now, how can that be?

VARCHI: I'll draw the proof from your own mouth, since you don't seem prepared to believe it when it comes from me.

TULLIA: Using what, the powers of logic?

VARCHI: You do like your jokes, and you enjoy poking fun at logic. "But she is in a blessed state and hears naught of it."[18] Indeed, you offend logic by your attitude. But logic itself will pay you back good for ill, first by letting you see, and then by forcing you to utter the truth at all costs.

TULLIA: Logic has not led me to any admission that cause and effect can be the same thing, nor will it do so, unless I first go mad.

VARCHI: What a fine tribute you pay to it! Logic alone is the reason that causes you to withhold that admission. Logic was invented for the discovery of truth and the disposal of falsehood, and anyone who uses logic for other purposes may be doing what he wants to, but is not doing what he ought to.[19] This kind of charlatan deserves the same punishment as a doctor who uses his science and skills not to heal the sick but to kill the healthy. Indeed, his punishment should be even harsher, because the soul deserves greater reverence than the body.

TULLIA: I'll tell you what I think: right now, you seem to be beating round the bush, as they say. Maybe it's because you're not too confident of being able to prove to my satisfaction what is impossible, or of making me say what I'm not prepared to admit.

VARCHI: Something that is quite impossible is clearly false and therefore cannot be shown to be true, nor would I try to prove its truth to you. Far less would I seek to make you say something you didn't want to, as this would be grossly discourteous and presumptuous. I'll try my utmost to prove to you, and induce you to affirm yourself, that what I said was quite true. So now, pray, what do you think "love" is?

TULLIA: Do you think you can just fire off a question like that and so suddenly to a woman, especially to a woman such as myself?[20]

---

18. Translation of "Ma ella s'è beata, e ciò non ode" (Dante *Inferno* 7.94).

19. That is to say, logic is a method, not a system. Varchi explained this at length in "Del metodo" (*Opere*, 2:797a and b especially).

20. Aragona is making an amused allusion to herself as an honest courtesan. The modern view that Aragona was hiding her profession is a misinterpretation of her actions and of sixteenth-century society. See p. 27 of the Introduction. See also what Tullia say of her experience in love on p. 75.

VARCHI: You are trying to get me to say that many women are of greater worth than a host of men. Perhaps you want me to touch on your own great merits, for you have always put more emphasis on decking out the soul with exceptional virtues than on embellishing the body with pretty or majestic ornaments. Yours is an attitude rare indeed at all times and worthy of the greatest acclaim. Actually, I didn't ask you what love was, but what you thought love was. For I am well aware that normally women's aptitude for love is feeble.

TULLIA: You're wrong there. Perhaps you were judging women's love from your own.

VARCHI: Imagine what you would have said if I had added (as I was on the point of doing) that women also love rarely and had quoted some lines from Petrarch:

"Whence I know full well that the state of love
Lasts but a short time in a woman's heart."[21]

TULLIA: Oh what a trickster you are! Do you think I can't see what you are up to? Just think what would have happened if Madonna Laura had gotten around to writing as much about Petrarch as he wrote about her: you'd have seen things turn out quite differently then! Anyway, why aren't you keeping your promise to me?

VARCHI: It's up to you, at this stage. You haven't yet told me what you think "love" is.

TULLIA: "Love," according to what I have frequently heard from other authorities, as well as by my own understanding of it, is nothing other than a desire to enjoy with union what is truly beautiful or seems beautiful to the lover.

VARCHI: That is most learned. Now how do you define "to love"?

TULLIA: It follows that "to love" is to desire to enjoy, and to be united with, either what is truly beautiful or what seems beautiful to the lover.[22]

VARCHI: Now can you recognize the difference that exists or, rather, that does not exist between "love" and "to love"?

TULLIA: I can recognize it. And I can see all the clearer that if logic teaches us such things, it must indeed be a holy pursuit! Nonetheless, I still fail to understand how the cause and the effect can be one and the same.

---

21. "Ond'io so ben ch'un amoroso stato / in cor di donna picciol tempo dura" (*Canzoniere*, 183.13–14).

22. Here Aragona gives a preliminary definition of love. It is a conflation of two separate statements by Leone Ebreo: "Love can correctly be defined as a desire to enjoy with union what is perceived to be good" and "Love is . . . desire of union . . . and union is the same as pleasure, for pleasure is nothing but the union with what is pleasurable, and the pleasurable is either what is good only, or beautiful as well, or seems beautiful to the lover" (*Dialoghi*, pp. 45, 364).

VARCHI: Be thankful to logic for saving you from falsehood! Anyway, from the definition of both "love" and "to love," you ought to have realized that, since both of them constitute an identical effect, they are bound to have an identical cause.

TULLIA: What, then, is their cause? And from what do they spring?

VARCHI: Don't you feel like hazarding a guess about that?

TULLIA: To be sure, I don't! Poets and philosophers have attributed so many different names to love, and excogitated so many mothers and fathers for it (although at times they deny love has any father), and they write about love under so many allegories, in so many fables and different guises, that I'd never be capable of guessing the truth of the matter or, indeed, what you take the truth to be.[23]

VARCHI: Just say what you yourself believe to be the truth, not what other people say.

TULLIA: Well then, for my part I believe that beauty is the mother of all forms of love.

VARCHI: Who, then, would be its father?

TULLIA: The knowledge of that beauty.

VARCHI: And how can I possibly refrain from praising you, Signora Tullia! Even so, you would have come even closer if you had stated that beauty is the father and knowledge is the mother, as we shall propose some other time. This derives from our conviction that the loved one is doubtless the agent, and consequently more noble, while the lover is the passive recipient, and therefore less noble, despite the contrary view which the divine Plato appears to hold on this distinction.[24]

TULLIA: Perhaps I erred in my spoken expression while my mind stayed on the right track. For I too consider, as I said a little earlier, that love is born

23. This is an allusion to Diotima's story in *Symposium*. In his commentary to Plato's work, Ficino introduces Plotino's allegorization of the myth (*Enneads*, 2.5.2–10 and 5.8.13), whereby Poros is a reflection of God and Penia is darkness or absence of divine light (Jayne, *Commentary on Plato's "Symposium,"* pp. 115–18). The epistemological and metaphysical meaning of the myth is discussed by Leone in *Dialoghi d'amore*, pp. 308–15. As to the poets' allegories, one need look no further than Sperone Speroni's *Dialogo d'amore* and the amusingly parodic story that the Tullia character attributes to the poet Molza. Since reason, divine gift to men, was corrupted by their base nature, Molza maintained, the gods have punished them by denying them a complete experience of love. In heaven the gods enjoy the amorous pleasures to the full, while only a reflection of love descends on earth, which nonetheless in human beings creates such thoughts as would raise them to heaven, if reason, with its practical considerations, did not turn them back to earth (*Trattatisti del Cinquecento*, 1:525–28).

24. Varchi's statement is in general agreement with Leone Ebreo's conclusion that the beloved is love's father, while the lover's mind, which becomes impregnated with the semen of what is beautiful, is love's mother (*Dialoghi*, p. 313). While running counter to Phaedrus' view in the *Symposium*, this interpretation is consistent with Diotima's view that the beloved is the principle of love (180, 204c).

from the knowledge and desire of beauty, both in the soul and in the intellect of the person who apprehends and desires it. But this seems a little far away from the doubt which sparked off our debate.

VARCHI: The subject of love is so vast, and its mysteries run so deep, that countless doubts are apt to beset each word we encounter, which may call for infinite treatment and learning. I realize that solely in order to define our question, we shall probably run out of time. So I'll go back to the beginning again and repeat that "limit" and "end" are the same thing and that whatever lacks a "limit" also lacks an "end." Conversely, whatever has no "end" can have no "limit." We also saw that "love" and "to love" are essentially, that is, in their essence, one and the same thing, despite the fact that they may seem to be different when the former is viewed as a noun, which signifies without time reference, and the latter as a verb, which gives a time qualification; but they are the same as far as their essence goes. In this sense, therefore, it may be asserted that "love" causes people "to love." Hence "loving" becomes the effect of "love." In the same way, we say that sight is the cause of seeing, hence seeing is called the "effect of sight," although "to see" and "sight" are in essence and in effect the same thing. So now it seems to me that the question that you initially proposed, as to whether it is impossible to love with a limit, has been resolved. Therefore I want you to maintain your promise and carry out your obligation, unless you are already exhausted, as I can imagine you might be.

TULLIA: You're the one who should be exhausted, indeed, and I almost said that you must be forgetful as well. You won't forget the promise . . .

VARCHI: What promise?

TULLIA: How can you ask that? You say that you have answered my question, when in fact the toughest and most rewarding part of the task lies ahead of us. I'm prepared to concede all that you have said up to this point, but it won't do you any good until such time as you can prove that love is without end. And that is something you are going to find very hard to do.

VARCHI: I spoke like that because of my wish to hear some of these gentlemen here do the talking, as well as the fact that I found very simple what you thought hard and obscure, maybe because you would like it to be so. Anyway, what reasons can you adduce to prove that love has an end?

TULLIA: No particular reason; but it is as I say.

VARCHI: So you want me to bow to authority!

TULLIA: No, Sir. I want you to bow to experience, which I trust by itself far more than all the reasons produced by the whole class of philosophers.[25]

VARCHI: So do I. But what experience would that be?

25. The idea that judgments ought to be based on experience goes back at least to Plato's *Republic* 9.382. Aristotle elaborates on it in several of his works, most extensively in *Metaphysics* 1.980 passim. Aragona, however, seems to be echoing Sofia's reply to Filone: "Your reasoning is no less plau-

TULLIA: Surely you know far better than I do that innumerable men, both in ancient and modern times, have fallen in love. Then, because of anger or some other feeling, whatever the reason might have been, they have stopped loving and jilted the women they had loved.

VARCHI: I wouldn't claim to know this better than you. However, yes, it is true that countless men, and countless women, both in antiquity and the present era, have been in love, and that then, whatever the reason may have been, they fell out of love, and many times their love turned into hatred, which is much worse.[26] So what do you wish to infer from this: that love has an end, and so one can love within a limit? I think you'd be deceiving yourself. However, since I know how intelligent you are and I can see you smiling away there, I'm sure you are trying to catch me out. I'll be satisfied if you acknowledge that I wasn't totally wrong, and also that I wasn't trying to be funny when I said at the outset that I didn't understand the terms of the debate. In fact, I never meant that kind of "end," and I don't believe that you had that "limit" in mind when you first laid the issue before me.

TULLIA: I will admit that much. Otherwise what I put up for discussion would not have been a debatable question but foolishness on my part, since it is obvious that people fall in and out of love at their own volition.

VARCHI: I would not like you to pass as foolish when in fact you are so clever, unless you're really trying to catch me out on this topic too. Actually, it is not quite as obvious as you suppose it to be.

TULLIA: Lord save us, you even want to argue the point on this one! I would certainly say . . .

VARCHI: What would you say?

TULLIA: . . . that you are quite the opposite of what I'm often told about you. Rumor has it that you decline to argue a single point with anyone, so people deduce that you are not very learned.

VARCHI: There are countless other signs and proofs that this is so,

---

sible than subtle; nonetheless, I base my judgment on experience, which we must trust more than any argument" (*Dialoghi*, p. 50). As to Varchi's pronouncements on experience, I have been able to find the following declarations: "Since everything can be proved either through authorities, or reasoning, or experience, we shall give precedence to authorities, which are held in much consideration by many; next to reasoning, which is greatly valued by philosophers; and, lastly, experience, which is opposed only by dolts" (from the lecture "Della generazione dei mostri," delivered in the Florentine Academy in 1548 [*Opere*, 2:673a and b]). In one of his lessons on love, Varchi wrote that experience is more valuable than reason and all the authorities put together (*Opere*, 2:538b).

26. The consideration that sensual pleasure may produce disgust will lead to the distinction between "vulgar" and "honest" love. Here the drift of the discussion parallels *Dialoghi*, pp. 44–53. Cf. note 55.

apart from my reluctance to argue, which is a significant pointer. But why invoke other proofs, if I myself refuse to deny it, and nobody states the contrary?

TULLIA: Please don't talk like that. For many people, and I am one of them, have taken up the cudgels on your behalf many times. Yet neither my defense nor that of any scholar, is really required in your case. For there is a quintessentially distinguished guarantor of all your virtues. We know the universally sound judgment of our virtuous prince, lord and duke, Cosimo de' Medici. We know how prudent, how understanding he is, and we may call him not merely illustrious, preeminent, and prosperous (for these are tokens of good fortune), but also a paragon of justice, character, and munificence. The Duke turns to you, and to your able pen, in matters worthy of everlasting memory.[27] Quite apart from the fact that the opinion of so eminent, wise, and virtuous a prince is indeed a crucial and infallible argument in your favor—which alone must grant you a great deal of satisfaction—we also know that this [habit of blaming the virtuous] is no modern failing. It rather goes back to antiquity, for Socrates, Plato, Aristotle and many other worthy men spent a major part of their time battling an entire generation of Sophists, as they were called, and were never completely able to silence them.

VARCHI: Nor indeed will they ever be silenced except by standing back from dispute and making fun of them. You should go back and read what happened in the old days to Cato, Seneca, Plutarch, and Galen. And then look how they treated Dante, Petrarch, and Boccaccio; in modern times the same thing has befallen Teodoro Gaza, Pontano and, to shorten the list, Longolio.[28] Or what happened to our Most Reverend Bembo just two days ago, to quote an outrageous example of such vexations.

TULLIA: Certainly Bembo is a perfect example, to say nothing about the other men: the goodness, doctrine, and refinement of that virtuous and erudite gentleman are endless. So he should be given homage, affection, and fame without end. He furthermore retains a breed of nobility that the common herd readily appreciates. He also has wealth, which is placed above all other merits by the common folk. It seems to be an unavoidable rule that the man who is praised and held in affection by people of worth, is sure to be blamed and held of no account by the others. However, let us leave them aside for the moment, as they are irrelevant to our present design. Please try and explain to me why it

27. This is a reference to the history of Florence that Duke Cosimo commissioned Varchi to write in 1545–46.

28. Teodoro Gaza was a Greek humanist who moved to Italy in 1442 and became famous for his Latin translations of Aristotle. Longolio is the Italianized form of Christoph Longueil, a Flemish humanist scholar who lived in Rome at the time of Leo X.

is neither so true nor so obvious, as I imagine, that one cannot love with a limit, taking the word "limit" in the other, and wider, sense.

VARCHI: Now we are moving too far away from the desired track. Yet I'm happy to follow it through for your sake. So tell me: suppose I ask you if one can live without eating, what answer would you give?

TULLIA: What a fine question! How do you think I would answer? I would say "Certainly not!" Provided the common run of men and women were not like that Scotsman in Rome in the time of Pope Clement, or that girl who is still alive in Germany and manages to survive without eating. So please don't think you can trap me with a half-swallowed mouthful!

VARCHI: Trust me. I'm doing some serious reasoning here. Not only do I find sophistic tricks distasteful, I actually have a mortal hatred for them. You gave a splendid answer, in fact. However, just let's suppose that somebody cited an instance, or lodged an objection, to show your opinion was wrong, and quoted the fact that the dead do not eat, how would you answer him?

TULLIA: Well, I'll leave you to be the judge of that!

VARCHI: Go ahead and say something.

TULLIA: Somebody is pulling my leg.

VARCHI: No, the jokes are coming from you. I've told you more than once, I'm taking each point seriously. I must insist that you give me a clear answer, or we will go on talking about something else, for I have a greater wish to hear these gentlemen speak and more need to learn from them than I have of doing the talking myself.

TULLIA: But I do not see what good it is for you to ask me why the dead do not eat. Everyone knows they no longer need to eat and they can't. In brief: they are defunct, no longer alive!

VARCHI: You see, you have said by yourself what you didn't believe when you heard it from me. What you ought to answer now is exactly this: just as the living cannot live without eating, so those who are in love cannot love with a set limit. If anyone adduced classical or contemporary examples, telling you that these and those characters, after falling in love, stopped loving and fell out of love, so to speak, you would have to confute them by saying: these people and those people were once alive and ate; now they are dead and no longer eat.

TULLIA: Ah, I see your point. What you mean is that while one loves, one does not love within limits. But when one no longer loves, the issue simply doesn't arise. This logic is truly manna from heaven! Now tell me: don't you believe there are some individuals who love, in order to achieve their own end, and then, when they have fulfilled that desire, love no more?

VARCHI: No, Madam.

TULLIA: You show yourself to be a little inexperienced in matters of love. Forgive me for pointing out that I have known a lot about such things, and still do.

VARCHI: I too know, and have known, the vicissitudes of love.

TULLIA: So what do you say?

VARCHI: I say theirs is no love, and they are not enamored.

TULLIA: They would insist that they are.

VARCHI: They do great wrong. They deserve a severe punishment.

TULLIA: Yes, they do, because they just end up leading poor, miserable women astray.

VARCHI: I don't blame them on that score, because there are also a number of women who play the same little game with men. Their real fault is that they give the most beautiful and precious label to what is just a vile and sordid act.[29]

TULLIA: You really don't give me any chances, do you? But I promise you, you will pay for it eventually! So come back to the proof that love is without an end and therefore lacks a "limit"—in the sense that we have agreed to use the term "end," in the present disputation. For if you can do this, I shall deem you a worthy hero indeed!

VARCHI: I don't intend to reply, because unfortunately you'll just try to score points against me. I know what you are like!

TULLIA: Yes, of course. Thank goodness you won't have much to say. And if you do have a response, speak up.

VARCHI: For that reason too I won't answer!

TULLIA: Please continue the discussion! As I said, you'll be a mighty hero, if you can prove to my satisfaction that love is without end.

VARCHI: Is it then such a heroic feat to defeat a woman?

TULLIA: You're not in a contest with a woman. You're fighting against Reason.

VARCHI: And isn't Reason female?

TULLIA: I don't know if it is female or male. Now let me do the talking for a while. Let's see if I can catch you by doing the questions my way. But don't hold it against me if I make a few blunders.

VARCHI: By all means, do begin. I shall answer correctly, and willingly.

TULLIA: If a thing has no end, is it infinite?

VARCHI: Without the slightest doubt.

29. Varchi's "vile and sordid act" is what Pausanias calls "common Aphrodite" or "love for the body," and what Ficino describes as a perturbation of the blood, a madness by which man sinks back to the nature of the beast (*Symposium* 181b; Jayne, *Commentary on Plato's "Symposium,"* pp. 158, 168; see also Pietro Bembo, *Gli Asolani*, ed. G. Dilemmi [Florence, 1991], p. 188).

TULLIA: Hence love, being without end (according to your own statement) is also infinite?

VARCHI: It must be. Who can doubt that?

TULLIA: Love, therefore, is infinite?

VARCHI: Come now, how many times do you want me to repeat it?

TULLIA: For your own good, I wish that you had never said it once, let alone gone on repeating it.

VARCHI: Why so? If I had thought you didn't like it, I wouldn't have said it.

TULLIA: The displeasure I feel springs from my affection for you. For in our discussions you have told me a thousand times that in the view of philosophers there is nothing infinite. This is because all things are finite. When I asked you the reason for it, you said that the infinite implies, denotes, and infers imperfection, precisely because it is infinite and so cannot be adequately grasped by any intellect. Would you venture to deny me this?[30]

VARCHI: I would, if it were false. But since it is true, I'll grant it. Indeed, I admit you are perfectly right.

TULLIA: Thank God that for once I have caught you in an error and you've confessed it with your own mouth.

VARCHI: What error can that be? And what exactly did I confess to?

TULLIA: You admitted that there is nothing infinite. Good God! do you want to go back on your words and deny it?

VARCHI: Not I, I don't want to deny that, for it's true. But I don't see why, because of that, you say that I am caught in an error.

TULLIA: Did you not say just a while back, that love has no end?

VARCHI: I said that.

TULLIA: And don't you affirm it any longer?

VARCHI: Yes, I do.

TULLIA: What a lucky stroke! I was beginning to have my doubts. And you still affirm that whatever has no end is necessarily infinite?

VARCHI: Yes, that too.

TULLIA: Therefore love, having no end, is infinite?

VARCHI: That necessarily follows.

---

30. Almost all ancient philosophers associated the idea of infinity with that of imperfection. Aristotle and his followers maintained that the infinite exists only potentially and in a qualified sense and that there are no objects that can be divided *ad infinitum*, or that are infinite in number or extent (*Physics* 3.204a2–208a4; *Metaphysics* 11.1–8). Tullia's and Varchi's discussion will lead to the distinction between infinite in potentiality and infinity in actuality. In a similar vein, in "Sopra alcune quistioni d'amore, Lezione quarta" (1554), Varchi will compare love to discreet quantity because it is capable of growing endlessly (*Opere*, 2:559a). For the date of the lecture, see *Lezzioni lette nell'Accademia Fiorentina raccolte nuovamente* (Florence, 1590), p. 385.

TULLIA: How can we reconcile the assertion that love is infinite with the fact that no one thing is infinite? I don't think we need too much logic here!

VARCHI: I agree.

TULLIA: So you will concede the point at last, just for once!

VARCHI: If I thought it would give you pleasure, I'd do much more than that to make you happy.

TULLIA: No, that's not a pleasure or a favor to me at all. It displeases me, in fact, and I would hold it against you. I can tell you, it would be a fine way of messing over me. In point of fact, I believe that, as the shrewd fellow that you are, you are now prepared to grant free of charge a point which you cannot barter. So go ahead and say it, if you have a valid response. Ha! I reckon this time I have trussed you up so tight that there isn't a single chink left that you can escape through.

VARCHI: If one is only looking for the truth, one is hardly concerned with escape routes.

TULLIA: Now I can look up to you as a man who tells the truth, and so what . . .

VARCHI: Wait, don't be annoyed with me yet. If you listen a bit longer and give me the replies that are relevant, you'll see that I don't merely have a few chinks to get me out from the logical quandary, but gaping windows and wide-open doors. So, I insist that you regard me as a man of truth.

TULLIA: I'll need Divine assistance, with all these retorts flying around me. You display more verbal subtleties than I have arguments to respond with. But I think that this time you're strutting around with nothing to back you up. So say what you want, and I'll answer you as best I can.

VARCHI: Isn't God infinite?

TULLIA: I knew that you would try to ambush me with this snare, but it won't help you, unless you are willing to dance round like a wooden puppet and show the double face of Janus.[31]

VARCHI: Have no fears on that score. I promise not to use any dishonest tricks of argument.

TULLIA: Tell me then, are you talking as a theologian or as a philosopher?[32]

---

31. The Roman diety, Janus Bifrons, guardian of gates, was depicted with two faces.

32. The belief that philosophy and religion had distinct aims and functions went back to the Middle Ages and was generally attributed to Averroës. Many philosophers, who thought reason to lead to unquestionable truths, bowed nonetheless to religion when the latter was in conflict with reason. This attitude came to be known as "double truth." Benedetto Varchi subscribed to this doctrine when lecturing on *Paradiso* I (*Opere*, 2:282–83). Bruno Nardi explains that, in essence, the practitioners of the double truth acknowledged that a great discrepancy existed between what

VARCHI: Whichever you like.

TULLIA: Come, tell me openly: in what capacity are you talking?

VARCHI: All right, as a philosopher.

TULLIA: Now you have really restored my confidence. Oh, I was so worried that you might give me a different answer. Soon enough you'll play into your adversary's hands.

VARCHI: As if I haven't been there a thousand times before! But what are you preening and squawking so much about?

TULLIA: I certainly used to believe, and I still do, in the theologians' affirmation that God is infinite. However, I had also learned that thinkers of the peripatetic persuasion, who are followers of Aristotle (as I assume you are), state that God is not infinite, on account of the fact that no single thing can be infinite in any location in the universe.[33] So now you've been surprised!

VARCHI: What do you mean by "surprised"?

TULLIA: Well, I mean that you shouldn't think of fobbing me off with any counterfeit arguments! Because you have stated that you were talking as a philosopher and not as a theologian. So now there will be no point in your abandoning the philosophers to take refuge among the theologians.

VARCHI: Why would there be no point for me?

TULLIA: See, I guessed what you were up to.

VARCHI: No, you didn't make a very good guess this time. For I was speaking, and continue to speak, as a follower of the Peripatetics. I can also assure you that you spoke with divine accuracy and that I'm holding the same beliefs and statements as you are. So what more could you want from me?

TULLIA: You always play it this way, showing me that I have won the argument at the outset, but then making me end up the loser.

---

can be understood by human reason and the truth that may be attained through the grace of God (cf. *Studi su Pietro Pomponazzi* [Florence, 1965], pp. 372–74). Leone Ebreo turned the argument around: "As long as faith is not in conflict with reason, we need no proof, for in that case it would not be faith, but science, and it is sufficient for us to believe what reason does not disprove" (*Dialoghi*, p. 240).

33. Here Tullia touches on a philosophical question that aligned on one side the Peripatetic philosophers, according to whom infinity can be conceived only theoretically in the sense in which numbers, bodies, and the possible intellect can be considered potentially infinite and, on the other side, the theologians, who believed in God's infinite creative power. Lecturing on *Paradiso* and on *Purgatorio* in 1564, Varchi made the following points: God is infinite only as far as duration is concerned; God can act only within necessary laws, not freely, because freedom signifies potentiality, that is imperfection; God did not create the world because no creation *ex nihilo* is possible (*Opere*, 2:323b, 348b). These ideas ultimately derive from Aristotle's *Physics* (1.291b13) and from Averroës's *Destructio destructionum*, trans. C. Calomino (Venice, 1527), 4.152. On God's infinite power, see Thomas Aquinas, *De Causis* 4. For Leone Ebreo on this subject, see footnote 38.

VARCHI: Don't you recall that old Florentine proverb that says: "he who wins the first round loses the whole fight"?

TULLIA: I can also think of another saying: "Saint John does not like tricks!"[34] It didn't particularly worry you to offer me the moon's reflection in a well. But to get back to the starting-point, according to the Peripatetics, there is no such thing as the infinite. And that means you are the loser.

VARCHI: In this game, there are never any losers.

TULLIA: So it's a bit like Valera's game.[35]

VARCHI: If you had let me finish, you would have seen that it's quite the opposite. At that game, nobody could lose, but here both sides are inevitably winners. For my part, I'd prefer to be a loser in this pursuit than a winner at other games. What I want to say, at any rate, is that any form of misunderstanding, or switching round the meaning of words, or not properly grasping the terminology in use, tends to cause a multitude of errors. Those who cannot understand words will never be able to understand anything. So our teachers ought to advise us far more carefully than they actually do, and when we debate we should always give an advance statement of the exact issue which we intend to discuss. Now, if we speak confusedly and in generalities as we have just been doing, then we can even maintain that, according to the philosophers, God is infinite.

TULLIA: Once again, I have the feeling you are trying to slip out of the argument, get away, and pay me with a song. In this view of the issue, I follow the Peripatetics . . .

VARCHI: So do I. When I say "philosophers," you can normally take it that I mean the Peripatetics.

TULLIA: I mean Aristotle.

VARCHI: I do too.

TULLIA: Then I'm stunned.

VARCHI: And I am staggered. Is there anyone who doesn't know that God has existed, and will exist, for all time?

TULLIA: What a stroke of genius! Everyone knows that God, having never had a beginning, will never have an end.

VARCHI: Therefore, He is infinite. What do you say to that?

TULLIA: You force my brain to such dizzy extremes! Give me a less elevated example, one that is a little bit clearer.

VARCHI: Doesn't Aristotle hold that time has always been in existence?

34. Saint John is the patron saint of Florence.

35. Translation of "ronfa del Valera." *Ronfa* was a popular card game. The proverbial Valera played a game that always ended in a draw.

Also, according to Aristotle, what has always existed can have no end.[36] Hence it will endure for ever. And as for something that never had a beginning, and will never have an end, wouldn't you call it "infinite?"

TULLIA: Yes I would. I reckon that it follows that motion must also be infinite, since time is simply the measurement of motion.[37]

VARCHI: That is well said. Quantity, too, will have to be considered infinite.

TULLIA: I wouldn't concede that so easily, because I can't fully grasp it.

VARCHI: Where there is motion—that is to say, movement—there is surely mobility: in other words some element that is being moved.

TULLIA: No doubt about that.

VARCHI: If movement is to be eternal, then what is moved must also be eternal.

TULLIA: Yes, Sir, indeed.

VARCHI: Hence, if the motion of the heavens is eternal, the heavens themselves must be eternal. Moreover, the heavens are corporeal, and all bodies are a "quantum." Therefore quantity, or rather magnitude, is eternal.[38]

TULLIA: I cannot gainsay these steps in the reasoning, so I am forced to believe it. But when I recall how often I have heard distinguished authorities declare that, according to Aristotle, God is not infinite, it all seems rather odd. I would ask you to rescue me from this maze of complexities by offering me a secret roll of string, like the one Ariadne gave to Theseus.

VARCHI: The best roll of string to effect your rescue is logic. Granted that this word "infinite" is a polyvalent term and can be interpreted in more than one way, and can carry different meanings, your preliminary step must be to state which of the meanings you intend to refer to. If you do this, it will be like lifting a heavy curtain from in front of your eyes. If those preliminary definitions are not posted, a person who declared that for the Peripatetics God is

36. What is referred to here is probably Aristotle's statement that, since time is a measure of change, what exists and does not change is eternal because it does not exist in time (*Physics* 4.221b4–6). In his lecture on *Purgatorio* 17 (1564), Varchi states: "those things that never had a beginning, cannot likewise come to an end" (*Opere*, 2:331b).

37. Cf. footnote 36. The Aristotelian *locus* for the concept of time and motion is *Physics* 4.218b21–9b11.

38. For the eternity of the world and the heavens Aragona could have drawn from Varchi's 1545 lecture on *Paradiso* I (*Opere*, 2:348b) or from Leone's *Dialoghi*, but the progression of her argument finds a closer parallel in the latter work. In *Dialoghi d'amore*, the opinions of Platonists, Aristotelians, and biblical theologians are considered methodically. Filone explains that, according to the Peripatetics, infinity can be conceived only inasmuch as time, motion, matter and the heavens connote processes traceable to infinity; hence God, being subject to the laws of necessity, cannot have created the world out of his own omnipotence, as the theologians say (pp. 136–39, 235–56). Cf. footnote 33.

infinite, would be as correct as the person who denied it, claiming that He is not infinite. Consequently, Aristotle provides us with this rule, that you should not begin a discussion with someone who uses undefined terminology, even if it is clear which definition of a term he is using, until he defines the meaning of his terms himself. That is why I didn't wish to reply to you at the outset, since I wanted to ask you first which meaning you had in mind.

TULLIA: Why didn't you do so?

VARCHI: Because you practically began by attacking me.

TULLIA: Then seize the opportunity to do it now.

VARCHI: I'll be happy to. Since this word "infinite" can stand for a plurality of different things, tell me, which of its various significations do you take in this debate?

TULLIA: You haven't understood my intention, and this has led you to further equivocation. What I intend is that you should make clear in what respect and in how many ways this word "infinite" can possibly be taken.

VARCHI: But that will lead us into an infinity of considerations. Nonetheless, here is what occurs to me on the spur of the moment, which should meet the purpose of the present discussion. Finite and infinite are essentially attributes or accidents of quantity. Quantity is of two types: continuous—which is also called magnitude or size—and discrete—which is also called multitude or number. Taking infinite in this sense, we cannot find anything anywhere in the universe that might be infinite in actuality. I say "in actuality" because, as nothing is infinite in actuality, so are all bodies infinite potentially, because they can be divided into an endless number of parts, and so *ad infinitum*. We, on the other hand, were considering what is infinite in actuality and not what is infinite in potentiality.[39]

TULLIA: Hold on a second, and tell me: aren't straight lines continuous in size?

VARCHI: They are.

TULLIA: Mathematicians in fact extend straight lines out into infinity.

VARCHI: Yes they do. However, mathematicians reason in abstract, not concretely, and we cannot comprehend, let alone conceive of such an infinity, not even in our imagination. As that may be, when they say *"ad infinitum,"* they postulate a lack of boundaries because it happens to suit their calculations.

TULLIA: Why is it impossible to conceive of the infinite?

VARCHI: Because the infinite is an indeterminable quantity, that is to say, a magnitude that has no limit, in other words, no end. So you can never take so

---

39. The concepts of actuality and potentiality are explained in *Metaphysics* 9.6.1048b.

many parts from it without leaving an infinite number of other parts that can still be subtracted. Hence our mind and intellect are bemused inside it.

TULLIA: I understand. However, even a discrete quantity seems infinite to me, because you would never be able to posit a number so large that I couldn't make it bigger, by adding a one, or any other figure I liked, to it.

VARCHI: Tell me, the figures that you are adding, are they finite or infinite?

TULLIA: They will be finite. But I'll add so many of them, that they will constitute an infinite number.

VARCHI: That is impossible, for we cannot derive anything infinite from what is finite. Therefore, numbers must be infinite not in actuality, but in potentiality. As continuous quantity may be divided and decreased *ad infinitum*, but never increased, so discrete quantity may be increased *ad infinitum*, but never decreased.[40]

TULLIA: How will you account for the human intellect, which is actuality and can, not only understand, but also be transformed into all manner of things and, therefore, is to be described as possible, as I have learned by reading one of your lectures?

VARCHI: You said it yourself that the intellect is everything in potentiality, not in actuality.

TULLIA: And yet it could be considered infinite, just like matter which can be molded into all kinds of forms and which, therefore, as far as I can judge, would be called infinite.

VARCHI: Matter not only is not infinite in act, but it is nothing at all. Nonetheless, it could be called infinite, like the intellect, that is, potentially, but only improperly so.

TULLIA: And what will you say about motion and time, which you called infinite earlier in our debate?

VARCHI: That they are infinite in time or, better, duration, because they are never all together, but always successively, by and by, one after the other. So their being in potentiality is mixed with their being in actuality.

TULLIA: I can easily see how matter is infinite, but I can't quite make out how God can be called infinite, as you were saying earlier.

VARCHI: Didn't I say that infinity, as such, cannot be understood? If you had not interrupted me, perhaps you would have understood better. Besides the meanings we mentioned, there is another infinite, what they call "infinite

---

40. Quantity can be either discreet, that is numerical, or continuous, that is geometrical. While discreet quantity may be increased to infinity, continuous quantity is divisible indefinitely (*Physics* 6.231b, 16–17; *Metaphysics* 11.3.1061a, 28). Cf. footnote 30.

of capability," that is, "of perfection," and philosophers call "of vigor" or "of power." With all this, no one will deny that God is infinite in regard to time or duration, having neither beginning nor end. Consequently, God is called "infinite" even by the Peripatetics. But they object to calling God infinite "of perfection" or, as we would say, "of capability" because, in that case, God would move the heavens not in twenty-four hours, but outside time, that is to say, suddenly and in a flash: for in one infinite capability or perfection, one would also find an infinite power. This consideration may be correct for the Peripatetics, but it is false in regard to the truth, as all theologians, as well as many philosophers, prove.[41]

TULLIA: Now I am really in possession of all the details! And I am on fire with such a passion for logic, that, if it is not too late for me to do so, I should like to devote myself to it night and day, and learn nothing else.

VARCHI: A big deal that would be for you! He who knows only logic, knows nothing at all.

TULLIA: Listen to this! It just makes me feel new all over! Haven't I often heard you say that without logic we can know nothing truly, because logic teaches us how to distinguish true from false, and right from wrong in all manner of things?

VARCHI: So you have, and it is true. Whoever has no logic and maintains that he knows anything at all, says what is not and cannot be.

TULLIA: So how do you resolve this contradiction?

VARCHI: Tell me, would you be able to say which lines are straight and which are crooked, without a rule or square?

TULLIA: No, I certainly couldn't.

VARCHI: And with more squares and plumb-lines than are available in the whole world, would you be able, without ever using them, to find out which wall is straight and which is not?[42]

TULLIA: No, Sir. But it would depend on me.

VARCHI: It would depend on you too, if you had more logic than has ever been thought of but strove after science without making the use of it for which it was devised. But let this be as it may, especially since there is much more to say about the question you have raised.

TULLIA: I think I have things clear without needing anything else coming from you.

VARCHI: In which way?

41. See footnotes 33 and 38.

42. "Being logic the instrument of all arts, nothing at all can be known without it, just as without rule or plumb-line nothing can be set straight, except by chance" from "Lezione una. Sopra il primo canto del *Paradiso*" (1545) (B. Varchi, *Opere*, 2:400a).

TULLIA: Love is infinite potentially—not in actuality—for it is impossible to love with an end in sight. In other words, the desires of people in love are infinite, and they can never settle down after achieving something. This is because after obtaining it, they long for something else, and something else again, and something more after that. And so it goes on, one thing after the other. They can never be satisfied, as Boccaccio bears witness about himself in the introduction to his *Decameron*.[43] This is the reason why people who are in love can be crying one minute and laughing the next. They can even be found laughing and crying at the same time. This phenomenon is amazing in itself and quite impossible for mere normal mortals! Lovers entertain both hope and fear. Simultaneously, they feel great heat and excessive cold. They want and reject in equal measure, constantly grasping things but retaining nothing in their grip. They can see without eyes. They have no ears but can hear. They shout without a tongue. They fly without moving. They are alive while dying. They say and do the myriad strange things that the poets write about, especially Petrarch, who towers incomparably over all others in the description of the pangs of love.

VARCHI: It is indeed true. But those people who do not have, and never had, experience of the effects of love, as I have and always shall, "If myself and my fancy I understand,"[44] will never believe it and will make fun of it. I know men who experienced love and later reproached it in others, thinking that they would never fall in love again or that they would not be able to. But then they fell in it deeper than before and paid for their pride and ingratitude. Love is god and a great god is Love. Those who are more able, and wiser than others, have always been loyal and obedient to the god. As to myself, I know Love's power well and I can bear strong and true witness to it. I wish it had not been so! In fact, I wish it were not so now! For I would not be as miserable and wretched as I am and I would not die a thousand times an hour, as I do and will by and by, for ever and ever; for love has no end nor limit whatsoever and feeds on lovers' minds, never to tire and become satisfied. But

"O grief! Why do you lead me out of my way,
And force me to say what I do not want to say?"[45]

You have made clear what I had no doubt about: namely, that you perfectly knew the solution to such a question. Although some reservations still linger in my mind.

---

43. In the foreword to the *Decameron*, Boccaccio says that the fire kindled in him by an uncontrolled amorous appetite made it impossible for his love to reach a satisfactory outcome.

44. Petrarch, *Canzoniere* 270.24.

45. Petrarch, *Canzoniere* 71.46.

TULLIA: If it is the case, as you say, that I have given a description of true love, then I am very sorry about it, because I would prefer the truth to be totally different from the way I've just described it, and, therefore, I'd like love to have an end. Now if you have a different view, speak out openly, for I shall be a very willing listener, as well as eager to be persuaded of the opposite case. And don't be worried on account of these gentlemen who are listening to us. In a general way, these matters concern all people, so everyone is happy to listen to them being discussed. You'll astonish us all the more, because we actually thought you were more skilled on other topics than love! We believed you'd be happier to speak about other subjects, since love was clearly outside your specific field; and also because you show character traits that are rather austere.

VARCHI: I would not know what I show outside and what I do not show. However, I will say this much: if I am aware of anything at all, I am aware of how little I know, for that is the one and first thing that I know. Everything else I know, I have learned from the voice of the living or the writing of the dead. This lesson alone I have been taught by the gods, by nature, and by Love, in a long and continuous experience. For I can say, from the day I was born—when Love began to hold me in his arms, a baby in swaddling clothes—until this very hour, past my forty-second year, I have never refrained from loving and never shall: and, as I always think of it, so do I wish to speak of it always. And despite the fact that many of us know that love is everywhere and governs all, we are unable to praise it as fully and as honorably as to come even close to its immeasurable worth.

TULLIA: To be honest, I myself took you to be such a person, and I have given clear proof of those sentiments, though many others refused to accept that you could be so and tried to convince me of the opposite. But tell me: what holds you back so that you do not talk and write of love more often, if not all the time?[46]

VARCHI: What holds me back is this very world of ours, where the names of things have been altered and the word "love," which is the noblest ever, is attributed to the vilest thing. Such is the confusion that, as soon as people learn that someone is in love, they immediately form an unfavorable opinion of him and, without any further consideration, make him out to be a debauched man, or, at the very least, a superficial and immature person. And apart from the fact that nowadays the title "philosopher" enjoys less prestige than would be fit-

46. In Padua, where he resided in 1539–41, Varchi lectured on Aristotle's *Ethics* and on a sonnet on jealousy by Bembo. The lecture was published in Mantua in 1545. By the time he met Aragona, Varchi had delivered lectures in the Florentine Academy on two sonnets and three songs by Petrarch, on Dante's *Purgatory* and *Paradise*, on alchemy and on colors. Cf. Pirotti, *Varchi*, pp. 18, 23. For the dates of Varchi's lectures, see *Lezioni sul Dante e prose varie*, ed. G. Aiazzi and L. Arbib. (Florence, 1841), I, viii.

ting, if we add to it the word "lover," no one among the general public would feel disqualified from ridiculing or teasing him.

TULLIA: Some people have in fact told me that you like to pass yourself off as a philosopher, but at heart you are not one.

VARCHI: This must be either because they misunderstand or because they do not know what "philosopher" actually means.

TULLIA: They really ought to know it, for they have had a distinguished mentor in you and also because I, a woman, am aware of it. So why is it that you write poems which deal with love and do not have such misgivings? Any person with that tendency or used to such behavior might tease you about it or even chastise you.

VARCHI: That happened to me once. I wish it had been of some good to me, as much as an inconvenience.

TULLIA: Why?

VARCHI: Because, if you write sonnets, people believe, besides other things, that you are capable of nothing and are good for nothing. They call you poet, thinking that this term is suitable for anyone who writes lines of verse, believing that it means nothing but a person full of nonsense and idle talk, not to say someone witless and crazy.

TULLIA: So why do you write sonnets?

VARCHI: Because about this matter, my attitude is different. I wish I had learned how to write sonnets! When, many years ago, I realized that it is not something for everyone to do—for it requires the knowledge of many subjects, besides intelligence and good judgment—I took myself out of it and never wrote sonnets again, especially after reading those penned by Monsignor Bembo; except, of course, when I was compelled to, or forced to reciprocate.[47] If I had trusted my talent, I would have paid no attention to what people say, as I never have in any other matter. If we offend no one but ourselves, so to speak, we must be allowed to do what we think best for us; for not all people value qualities and reputation equally and in the same manner. So, if we do not like to be criticized, we ought to do nothing at all.

TULLIA: Indeed, those are very odd opinions to hold. Don't such detractors know that Petrarch enjoys immense prestige and has a renown equaled by none other and more so because of his poetic compositions than anything else?

VARCHI: What do you suppose such people think of Petrarch? But now let us talk about something else.

---

47. Varchi's poetic production consists mainly of sonnets, and the majority of them are sonnets of correspondence. In his lifetime, his verse production appeared in print twice, in 1555 and 1557.

TULLIA: Please let's: "For to want to hear this is a base desire . . ."[48] and, as Dante said about the cowards: "Let us not speak of them; just glance, and pass on."[49] But now I'd prefer you to propose those doubts that you mentioned earlier.

VARCHI: I was joking.

TULLIA: No, you were not making jokes. I know you well too well for that, apart from the fact that you have often repeated on your own account that you never joke in such matters.

VARCHI: So finally you have concluded that love is infinite, hence one cannot love within limits, since lovers have always new desires and are never satisfied with whatever result they attain without longing for something more. Isn't that so?

TULLIA: Perfectly true.

VARCHI: Now against this conclusion of yours, I argue thus: "All rational agents—that is, all those who act with cognition—do what they do in order to reach a certain end." What do you think of this proposition?

TULLIA: I concede the proposition because I know it comes from Aristotle. But I'd like to know the reason for it.

VARCHI: The reason is that nothing moves to do anything by itself, but must be moved by something else. And, as the Philosopher says, the end is what moves the agent.[50]

TULLIA: I'll believe it, because it comes from the Philosopher, but I'd like to know the reason for that assertion too.

VARCHI: I know that you do not want to budge without being budged. The reason is that nothing can operate by itself, either in body or in spirit, but needs an external agent, that is, something outside itself that moves it.[51]

TULLIA: I also believe this. I'd like to ask you the reason for that too, but I'm afraid I might seem a nuisance, or annoy you, and in any case it would lead us on to endless complications.

VARCHI: Do not fear, for in all things one comes back to the head or principle which is known in itself. Being first, it has nothing before itself; being known, it needs no declaration. As for me, nothing can be bothersome if it pleases you. Moreover, whoever strives after the reason of things will never seem importunate to me; anyone who does not so seek, is far too negligent.

---

48. Dante, *Inferno* 30.148.

49. Dante, *Inferno* 3.51.

50. *Metaphysics* 11.1–8; *Physics* 2.194a–25–30; 198b1–9; 8.267a6–8. The expression "the end moves the agent to act" is in Aquinas' *Summa contra Gentiles* 1.37.

51. *Physics* 8.254b7–6a3.

TULLIA: Tell me then why no single thing can set itself in motion.

VARCHI: Because the result would be self-contradictory and outright impossible. The same thing would be moving and the cause of its moving; or, if you prefer, the same object would act and be acted upon.

TULLIA: And why is that self-contradictory and impossible?

VARCHI: You are trying my patience. Because the same thing would be in actuality and in potentiality at the same time: which is, indeed, outright impossible!

TULLIA: You are a thousand times right, but I don't see how being right on this could help you with the problem of the Prime Mover.[52]

VARCHI: This would also be valid for the Prime Mover. But let us not rise to such heights now. Do you concede that whoever moves, moves to some end?

TULLIA: Yes, I can concede that too.

VARCHI: I further maintain, following another of Aristotle's propositions, that "all things that move to some end, stop and no longer move as soon as that end is reached."[53]

TULLIA: That seems reasonable, because otherwise things would spin out *ad infinitum*. But what has this to do with it? It appears that you are right, but on a point that is irrelevant.

VARCHI: You will see very soon. The relevance of it is that whoever longs for something, as soon as that something is attained, longs no more.

TULLIA: I'm beginning to understand your line now, and I can see what you want to get to, but I don't believe you'll reap the benefit. Now come to your conclusion.

VARCHI: I have almost concluded. Once you concede the two premises (the major and the minor, which make up the syllogism, as the logicians say), then you must, whether you like it or not, concede what follows, that is to say, come to the conclusion.

TULLIA: So please draw your inferences and state the conclusion of this syllogism.

VARCHI: If all lovers have an end in mind, and if all those who reach their end no longer move, that is, cease from their purpose, it necessarily follows that all lovers who attain their aim become satisfied and no longer love.

---

52. Aristotle's prime mover initiates the motion of the universe without itself being moved (*Physics* 8.256a4–8b9; 258b10–260a19).

53. Leone writes that love is the beginning of motion: "desire is the soul's movement toward the object of desire and love is the soul's movement toward the beloved. Pleasure is the cause of this motion called love and desire" (*Dialoghi d'amore*, p. 210). Perhaps Varchi is referring to Aristotle's statement that "an object ceases moving when the mover ceases causing it to move" (*Physics* 8.267a6–8).

TULLIA: That is undeniable.

VARCHI: Hence, love has an end, and it is therefore possible to love within limits. So the conclusion you reached earlier was incorrect.

TULLIA: No, I drew that conclusion correctly, and it was easy enough to do so, and anyone could have come to it. However, you were the one who set up the premises, which is what the thrust of the argument turns on. You need not believe that I'm talking like this because I've changed my stance and think your objection to be false now, when in fact I hold it to be perfectly true. Indeed, as I accept it as the proof, I am bound to believe it. And I could never change my mind and start thinking that matters stand differently, if what you have told me on other occasions is correct: namely, if a person comes to know something by proofs and knowledge, he can never subsequently change his mind and disbelieve it. Hence, since this and that conclusion are both perfectly correct, I am forced to hold them both to be true, and I do so. So I can answer thus: no lover ever accomplishes his final goal, for if he did, what you have just concluded about love having to cease would be the absolute truth.

VARCHI: You speak beautifully, with order and erudition. However, it will be very easy for me to prove what is well known to everyone and what you yourself admitted only a short while ago when you stated that many ancient as well as modern men have first loved and later forsaken their love. Among so many people, we must believe that at least one of them enjoyed that pleasure which is so great that no other is greater, as Boccaccio puts it.[54]

TULLIA: This time you have surely cut the ground out from under your own feet.

VARCHI: I would not be the first one to shoot down my own pigeons. But tell me why.

TULLIA: Because this word "love," since it can stand for various types of loving, is a polyvalent noun. And you didn't ask me first what kind I meant.

VARCHI: Ah, Signora Tullia, you have got me there!

TULLIA: You asked for it; it's your loss.

VARCHI: I admit it. So I ask you now what kind of love you had in mind.

TULLIA: Indeed, I am going to tell you. Leaving all possible subdivisions aside, let me say that love is of two types. We shall call the first "vulgar" or "dishonest" love, the other "honest," that is to say, virtuous. Dishonest love—which is found only in vulgar and low-minded individuals, that is, in those whose souls are low and vile, who lack virtue or refinement, whether they

54. Varchi, that is, Aragona, is presumably paraphrasing the nun's words: "I have often heard from many women who come to see us that all the pleasures in the world are hollow in comparison with what a woman feels with a man" (*Decameron* 3.1, 23).

come from noble or insignificant stock—is generated by a desire to enjoy the object that is loved, and its goal is none other than that of common animals. They simply want to obtain pleasure and to procreate something that resembles themselves, without any further thought or concern. Those who are moved by this desire and who love in this guise, as soon as they have reached their goal and have satisfied their longing, will desist from their motion and will no longer love. As a matter of fact, they may quite often recognize that they have made a mistake, or get fed up with the time and trouble they have put into it, and so they turn their love into hate. Of course, I was not considering this type of love.[55]

VARCHI: I certainly believe you, for I know that your noble heart would never stoop so low as even to think of talking about such vile matters. But pray go on.

TULLIA: Honest love, which is characteristic of noble people, people who have a refined and virtuous disposition, whether they be rich or poor, is not generated by desire, like the other, but by reason. It has as its main goal the transformation of oneself into the object of one's love, with a desire that the loved one be converted into oneself, so that the two may become one or four. Many times this transformation has been beautifully described by Petrarch, as well as by the Very Reverend Cardinal Bembo.[56] And as this transformation can only take place on a spiritual plane, so in this kind of love, the principal part is played by the "spiritual" senses, those of sight and hearing and, above all, because it is closest to the spiritual, the imagination. But, in truth, as it is the lover's wish to achieve a corporeal union besides the spiritual one, in order to effect a total identification with the beloved, and since this corporeal unity can never be attained, because it is not possible for human bodies to be physically merged into one another, the lover can never achieve this longing of his, and so will never satisfy his desire.[57] Thus, he cannot love with a limit, as I con-

---

55. The distinction between two types of love is a commonplace of Renaissance literature on love. Aragona, however, seems to have drawn directly from *Dialoghi*, where Filone distinguishes the desire for the pleasurable, which ceases when satisfied (16, 18, 47–48), from the "perfect love between man and woman," which is everlasting (50–51). The idea that satiety removes desire— "these [carnal] pleasures have such peculiarity that once obtained, the longing for them subsides, and not only does love very often cease altogether, but many times it turns into vexation and hatred"—is scattered throughout Leone's work (pp. 16, 18–19, 47–48, 51).

56. Petrarch, *Canzoniere* 15.10–11; 73.85–86; 94.6–8, 11–13; 242.12–14. The conceit is found in most sixteenth-century collections of poetry.

57. Aragona's explanation of the permanent character of good love is drawn from *Dialoghi d'amore*: "Although the lover's appetite is satisfied by copulation, and his carnal desire instantly ceases, nonetheless his heart's yearning is not thereby diminished. . . . When the lovers are united in spiritual love, their bodies also wish to enjoy such union as is possible . . . so that their coming together may be in all respects complete, especially because through a corresponding bodily

cluded earlier. Although one could extend the description of these two types of love indefinitely, I consider what I have said sufficient to demonstrate that my conclusion is entirely valid.

VARCHI: Everything you said has pleased me highly and filled me with ineffable sweetness. And although I have a few reservations left about what you said, still they are very minor ones. Above all, I was gratified to see that not only have you read Filone, but you have also understood and retained what you read.[58]

TULLIA: Oh, please, if you are truly fond of me, do me a favor, since you have mentioned Filone, and give me your considered opinion of his work.

VARCHI: Please do not insist, because people have their own opinions and pretensions.

TULLIA: But that is precisely what I want to draw out from you.

VARCHI: Don't bother, if you love me.

TULLIA: Why?

VARCHI: Because my habit is to speak freely, and I cannot help saying what I think, while nowadays it is not customary to behave in this manner— indeed one should not. If people hear about it, I can well imagine what many will say.

TULLIA: The more you deny me this favor, the more I find that it appeals to me. We are among friends here, in a virtually private setting, and nothing that may be said is going to be bruited abroad, so please go ahead and tell me your opinion, as I have begged you.

VARCHI: I guess I must sink or swim! Of all the authors, whether ancient or modern, who wrote about love in any language, I prefer Filone. I think I have learned more from him than from anybody else, for he speaks about love not only more comprehensively, in my modest opinion, but with more doctrine and more truthfully.[59]

---

consummation, spiritual love increases and becomes more perfect." To a diffident Sofia, Filone sets out the reasons why his good love for her will endure: "Such love is desire for a complete union of the lover and the beloved, and this can come about only with the total penetration of one into the other. This is possible for souls, which are spiritual, for spiritual and incorporeal entities can interpenetrate and become one, with most efficacious results. But when separate bodies are concerned, which require specific positions in space, after their penetration there remains, in comparison with the consummation that is desired, an even more ardent longing for that union that cannot be perfectly brought about (49–50, 56). On Aragona's definition of love and her use of Leone's theory, see my Introduction, pp. 30, 35, 39.

58. By "Filone," Tullia refers to Leone Ebreo's *Dialoghi d'Amore*, whose speakers are Filone and Sofia.

59. Benedetto Varchi praised Leone Ebreo's work in a more qualified way than does the Varchi character here. "If Leone Ebreo's *Dialogues* were clothed [in the language] they deserve, they would lack nothing for which to envy Latin or Greek authors." "Recently, Filone Ebreo's three books of

TULLIA: Have you included Plato in your reading and the *Convivio* by Signor Marsilio Ficino?[60]

VARCHI: Yes, Madam, I have and I think they are both marvelous. But Filone pleases me more, perhaps because I do not understand the others.

TULLIA: This is high praise.

VARCHI: It would be, if the praise were given by someone competent to judge, and if other [writers] had not come first.

TULLIA: Enough then, for I too held that opinion, until someone told me that a number of Filone's doctrines were not peripatetic, so I left off reading his work.

VARCHI: You were wrong there. In Plato too you will find statements that are not peripatetic in character. In any case, if we want to judge a book properly, we must consider its contents overall. But let us allow people to judge for themselves, and let them have the freedom we would like to allow ourselves, that of expressing our opinions freely. Behaving this way, we shall not deceive anyone who does not want to be deceived; each one is free to believe it, if he knows something about it, or to ask someone else, if he does not understand. On the other hand, if someone thinks he understands, while he does not, it is as good as if he did, and it would be foolish to disabuse him. Many have written a great deal about love, some learnedly and some in a delightful manner, others in both ways. To all I prefer Filone—although on some points, especially in what concerns the Jewish faith, I excuse more than approve of what he says. I am not referring to those who have spoken about love not as it is, but as they themselves have experienced it, or as they would like it to be, and have described not love's nature, but rather their own character and the character of their women. But let us discuss this on some other occasion, for this subject is such that no matter how much we have said about it, there is always far more to say. As to me, I could never be satiated or get tired of talking about it, but I must not annoy you people here.

TULLIA: It seems that you don't know us very well. You've astonished us. For myself, when you made all those excuses, I thought you might be blaming Filone, at first. Then when I heard you give him that glowing praise, I felt convinced, and I'll wager that all these gentlemen with us were convinced, that you wanted to make a reference elsewhere.

---

dialogues came to light. Matters of love are thereby treated so extensively and truthfully, albeit in an obscure or confusing way, that I prefer his books to any other." "Filone Ebreo, whom, in my judgment, one can believe as any other" (*Opere*, 2:155, 536a, 536b).

60. By *Convivio* is meant Marsilio Ficino's *Commentarium in Convivium Platonis de Amore* (1469). The Italian translation, done by the author in 1474, appeared with the title of *Sopra lo amore o ver' Convito di Platone*.

VARCHI: Where?

TULLIA: You're asking me, then? To *Gli Asolani* by our Most Reverend Bembo, and not to Filone's *Dialogues*.

VARCHI: What made you think so?

TULLIA: The fact that Bembo's work deserves great praise from all manner of people, and also because here there is no one who is unaware of the unprecedented affection that you have felt, over a number of years, for His Most Reverend Eminence.

VARCHI: I harbor the greatest love and respect not for Bembo but for his goodness. I admire and worship not Bembo but his virtues, which I never sufficiently praised as to believe I had praised them adequately. Mind you, I do not deny that the *Asolani*—which I have extolled a thousand times—are splendid and that a very sound judgment and a miraculous eloquence are combined with his great doctrine. Filone, on the other hand, had a different aim. In love's taxonomy, more—I think—can be said and perhaps in more charming style, but I do not think it could be said better. But, pray, do not let it be known outside these walls, for people might start murmuring that I have changed my views and betrayed Bembo.

TULLIA: Don't worry about that. Let's return to our main discussion: tell me the doubts that my statements raised in your mind.

VARCHI: Did I not tell you that they were not very important? And I am afraid I do not remember them now. Besides, it is getting late, we are keeping these gentlemen waiting, and there might not be sufficient time to hear those others who have not uttered one word all day long.

TULLIA: Don't get so worked up about things, and stop worrying, because those were our plans. Just continue with your argument.

VARCHI: I shall no longer deny you anything at all, for in the end I always grant you everything. First of all, I do not understand why you blame and call "dishonest" that kind of love that is not only common to all animate things—I mean earthly creatures—but is proper to them, for they are made more for it than for anything else. We can observe this in plants and grasses, which have a vegetative soul; in all brutish animals, which have vegetative and sensitive souls; and in human beings as well, who possess a rational or intellectual soul besides the vegetative and the sensitive ones. For Aristotle says that the man who cannot generate, since he cannot do what nature has created him to do, is no longer a man.[61] Secondly, I wonder what you would say about those men

---

61. The nearest source I could find for this dictum is Thomas Aquinas's expression "it is a sign of a thing perfection that it is able to produce its like," apparently quoted from Aristotle's 4 *Meteor* (*Summa contra Gentiles* 1.37).

who love boys, whose urge cannot obviously be a desire to generate something similar to themselves. Furthermore, it does not seem true that all those
who love with a vulgar and lascivious love desist from loving as soon as they
have satisfied their desires; on the contrary, there are many who seem to burn
more ardently afterwards. These three points I have raised in regard to the first
type of love are enough for the time being.

TULLIA: These are not casual objections, or points of slight importance,
as you made them out to be. I know that you like to conduct a detailed analysis of everything. But I'll reply to the best of my ability. I would answer your
first point by saying that I am well aware that we humans cannot be repre-
hended, or praised, for the instinctive drives that arise from our nature. Hence
the first type of love is not to be blamed, either in the plant or the animal kingdom. And it should not be called lascivious or "dishonest" in them, or indeed in
human beings. Rather, it can be and should be lauded to a greater extent in humans because they are capable of generating offspring of a more noble and
worthy caliber than plants and animals can. My main proviso is that this appetite should not become unbridled and overpowering, for this often happens
with human beings, who are endowed with a free will, while it does not occur
in the plant or animal kingdom. It is not just because animals are animals—as
an Empress once replied in a famous aside—but because they are guided by an
unerring mind. Hence, since no one deserves censure for eating and drinking,
but rather should be congratulated, because these processes restore the natural warmth and essential humors which maintain us in life, so people should
be praised, and no one censured, for generating offspring that are similar to
themselves, thus perpetuating themselves in the species, since they cannot reproduce themselves as individuals. However, just as we can blame and also
chastise someone who eats or drinks more than is reasonable, or at the wrong
place and time, in a way that things that were supposed to benefit him actually
harm him, so we ought to chastise and blame far more vigorously those persons who yield to the passions of the flesh without due limit and moderation.
For in doing so, they subordinate reason, which ought to be the queen of the
body, to the senses, and thus they quickly turn from being rational men into
being brute animals.[62] Another argument comes from the venerable hermit of
Lavinello, who used to say that nature would have inflicted too great a wrong
on us, and been far more cruel than a stepmother, if we were only ever in a position to venture our capital at a loss and could never make a gain.[63] For just as

---

62. The direct source for Aragona's distinction between natural love and human love is probably
Purgatorio 17.91–111 and 18.49–66. It is dealt with by Aquinas in *Summa theologica* 1.60.1–3 and
goes back to Aristotle's *Nichomachean Ethics*. In Bembo's *Gli Asolani*, the distinction is voiced by
Lavinello in book III.

63. *Gli Asolani*, pp. 200–201

brute animals can never be transformed into plants, while we humans can become animals, under no circumstances can animals ever change into human beings, whereas we humans can aspire to become angels by way of love. Therefore we can never sufficiently blame—for our criticism would always fall short of his error—anyone who lowers himself by way of dishonest love from the level of human beings, which is perfect, to the level of wild beasts. Equally, it is hard to find enough praise for anyone who rises by way of divine love from the human plane to that of the immortal gods. Yet what further exposition of this point is needed, since it has been discussed with such eloquence and learning by that venerable divine whom I mentioned earlier? For my part, I can never read the words of that saintly hermit without feeling myself somehow elevated from the ground and transported to the heavens amidst such sweet sounds and ineffable chants, such rejoicing and bewilderment, that I can't explain the experience, nor could anyone else believe it if they had not experienced it.

VARCHI: You need not strive so hard to persuade me, Signora Tullia, for it has the same effect on me, perhaps a stronger one.

TULLIA: I can imagine so, because you understand it more fully and relish it more sharply.

VARCHI: I did not mean that.

TULLIA: No, I am saying it myself! But we'll come now to the second of the points you raised. Here I consider that those men who entertain a lascivious love for youths are not following the true dictates of nature, so they fully deserve the punishments that canon and divine law have imposed on them, as well as the penalties set up by man-made and civil justice. What is more, I can scarcely believe that people who practice such an ugly, wicked and hideous vice, whether an artificial or habitual form of behavior, are real human beings. I shall be glad if later on you could give me your own view on this, for I know full well that in classical Greece the opposite notion was common and that Lucian wrote a dialogue in which he praised this vice, as did Plato.[64]

VARCHI: I want to reply to you now instead of postponing this question until later, for you are mixing things up and taking logs for axes. You are greatly mistaken if you compare Lucian with Plato, and if you furthermore believe that Plato praised such filthy wickedness. For God's sake, get such an ugly belief, such grievous sin, out of your head, for it is unworthy of a person of the lowest mind, let alone of your very gentle soul.

TULLIA: Do forgive me. I had understood that not only did Socrates and

64. This is a reference to Plato's *Symposium* and *Phaedrus*. Lucian's panegyric of homosexual love can be found in *Affairs of the Heart* (*Amores*), ed. and trans. D. MacLeod, Loeb Classical Library (Cambridge, MA: Harvard University Press: 1967), 8.150–235.

Plato make a public spectacle of their affairs with young men, but they also took it as something to be proud about, and they wrote dialogues, as we can see in the cases of Alcibiades and Phaedrus, where they speak about love with great beauty and passion.[65]

VARCHI: I do not say that Socrates and Plato did not show their love for youths in public, that they were not proud of it and did not speak of love with great beauty and passion. I simply maintain that they did not love them the way that people commonly interpret and apparently you also believe.[66] I'll say more: I do not know who speaks more amorously about love than Solomon in his "Song of Songs."[67]

TULLIA: I'll take what you say on trust. But do tell me, were they in fact lovers?

VARCHI: Of course they were lovers! Very much so.

TULLIA: So were they desirous of generating something resembling themselves?

VARCHI: Do you doubt it?

TULLIA: I don't quite know how to respond. You have a way of turning everything around against me. Yet I am sure that, in that case, they could not achieve their goal. Indeed, no one can reasonably long for things that cannot come to pass, and which they cannot possibly obtain.

VARCHI: You customarily appear to be more attentive and of better mind and judgment than you seem today. I am beginning to suspect that all of you here are setting me up to see how far I will go. What makes me sure of it is your keeping so quiet, no matter what I say. I am aware that you know that, just as pregnant bodies long to generate, so do pregnant souls, and even more so. Socrates and Plato, therefore, whose souls were replete with all goodness, overflowing with doctrine, rich in all virtues and, finally, pregnant with all kinds of lofty and venerable habits, desired nothing more than giving birth and generating something similar to themselves. Those who deny it, or believe otherwise, do not describe Socrates and Plato; they rather give themselves away. This is the real and authentic virtuous love. It is as much worthier than the other as the soul is worthier than the body. These lovers deserve far

---

65. Phaedrus eulogizes homosexual love and Alcibiades tells of his attempts at seducing Socrates (*Symposium* 178b–180b; 215–19).

66. The misreading of Phaedrus' and Alcibiades' eulogies by the Varchi character is consistent with the interpretation that the real Varchi gives of *Symposium* in "Sopra alcune quistioni d'amore. Quistione prima" and is reflected in the justifications he gave when caught in amorous pursuit of young pupils (for Varchi's homosexual loves, see Pirotti, *Varchi*, pp. 47–53).

67. In *Dialoghi d'amore*, the "Song of Songs" is read as the ecstasy of the soul united with God (p. 355).

more praise than the others, just as generating a beautiful soul is far more commendable than giving birth to a beautiful body.[68] Do not be deceived by today's customs: be satisfied by knowing that procreators of this type are to be commended, and the more so for not being generally appreciated. But we are treading on very difficult ground, and besides you know everything already. So, do go back to your third question.

TULLIA: I wouldn't like to let that point slip by in such a hurry. Despite my awareness that what you are saying is perfectly true, I should still like to know why a woman cannot be loved with this same type of love. For I am certain that you don't wish to imply that women lack the intellectual soul that men have and that consequently they do not belong to the same species as males, as I have heard a number of men say.[69]

VARCHI: It was someone's belief—but it is far from the truth—that the difference between men and women is not one of essence. And I myself maintain that not only is it possible to love women with an honest and virtuous love, but that one ought to. As far as I am concerned, I know those who have done it and do it all the time.

TULLIA: You have quite restored my confidence! But please tell me, what is the significance of the fact that these Socratic lovers tend not to love those who are unprepossessing, or simply too old?[70]

VARCHI: I thought I was the one who always wanted to split hairs. Who told you this?

TULLIA: I can see it every day with my own eyes.

VARCHI: Would to God that these lovers we are talking about were as commonly found as they are rare, or that one of them were to be seen at least once in ten years, if not every day. What you say is quite true: the most beautiful people, or those who seem most beautiful, are loved more than the others, and they are loved more up to a certain age than later.

TULLIA: And what could be the reason for that? Please don't quote me the reasons that monks commonly put forward when they try to exculpate themselves.

VARCHI: If these reasons are true and persuasive, why should I not put them forward?

68. Varchi presents Socrates' view of love for the good, as per *Symposium*, 205d and 206d and Ficino's *Commentary*, p. 54. As I pointed out in footnote 66, he does not differentiate between Socrates' speech and those preceding it.

69. For the misogynistic implications of "Socratic" love, see the Introduction, p. 37.

70. "Socratic love" is the expression used by Ficino throughout his *Commentary* to signify love for the beautiful. The famous expression "Platonic love" was used for the first time in his letter to Alamanno Donati in 1476–77 (Sears Jayne in Ficino's *Commentary*, p. 174, note 4).

TULLIA: Maybe by hearing them from your own lips I'll be tempted to accept them.

VARCHI: First of all you ought to realize that one may not understand or get to know anything at all except through one's senses, and that, of all the senses, the noblest and most exquisite is sight.

TULLIA: I know and can concede all that. But you're starting off at a very high plane and from propositions that are universal.

VARCHI: When I am with you, I am forced to proceed in this fashion, for you are always picking holes in things and want to find out the whys and wherefores of everything. Since the good and the beautiful are the same . . . [71]

TULLIA: I didn't know that and I don't concede it. Otherwise, following this line, we could say that all beautiful people are virtuous.

VARCHI: You well know . . .

TULLIA: Be careful, don't be deceived. For myself, I have met many handsome people, but they weren't at all virtuous for that.

VARCHI: So have I. Nonetheless what I say is true, for these people have turned out to be the way they are, not because of their nature but by accident, either through their fathers' fault or their teachers' incompetence or their friends' failing. Remember the proverb "Bad company will teach you bad ways," for it is very true. I furthermore can say that these people, when they are bad, are worse than others, in fact they are evil.

TULLIA: I beseech you to tell me the reason for that.

VARCHI: This is the way nature works. If something is better and perfect in its natural essence, it becomes worse and more flawed whenever it spoils, corrupts, and loses its essential purity. So it follows that, while we cannot find a more blessed, benign, and useful animal than the human animal, when good, by the same token there is none as bad and wicked, malicious and harmful, when bad. If you wish for a more concrete example remember that, as the saying goes, it is the sweetest wine that produces the strongest vinegar.

TULLIA: I like that. But please continue with your syllogism.

VARCHI: My syllogism is good and ready. If it is the beautiful people that are loved, it is because they are usually judged not only the best but of higher

---

71. For the relation between the beautiful and the good, see *Symposium* 201, 205d, 206d; *Commentary*, p. 49. Tullia's and Varchi's conversation seems to follow the guideline provided by *Dialoghi d'amore*. In Leone's work, too, the comparison between the beautiful and the good brings about the distinction between opposites and contraries: what is not beautiful is not necessarily ugly; fair and foul are contraries, not opposites, therefore they are not incompatible, for there is a mean between them (pp. 224–26). The Aristotelian *locus* for the concepts of opposites and contraries is *Categories* 10.2b. Varchi dealt with these topics in his "Third doubt: whether the good ones are also beautiful" (1554) (*Opere*, 2:528).

intelligence, and it ought to be so, except in the cases I mentioned earlier. I say this only because—believe me—I personally judge it to be so and hold it to be the truth. If I behaved in any other way, I would play into the hands of those who contend that I am no philosopher.

TULLIA: That's fine. So now, if we follow your rule of contraries, all those people who are ugly must be wicked.

VARCHI: No, Madam.

TULLIA: What do you mean by "no"? Surely beautiful and ugly are contraries?

VARCHI: They are and they are not.

TULLIA: That seems to me a clear contradiction in terms, but I won't go into it any further since I am obviously not learned in logic. You tell me how the contradiction can be cured.

VARCHI: It is quite easy. Contraries can be of many kinds. The rule I am considering applies only to contraries of exclusion, not those of inclusion.

TULLIA: I can't follow that.

VARCHI: "Contraries of inclusion" are those that signify two contrary natures, such as "white" and "black," "sweet" and "bitter," "hard" and "soft," and the like. The rule does not apply here, because not everything non-white is black, nor is everything that is not sweet bitter, and so forth. "Opposites of exclusion," on the other hand, do not indicate two different natures, but, rather, one indicates one nature and the other the lack of that nature, as we have in "alive" and "dead," "night" and "day," "sighted" and "blind," and other such contraries. With these, the rule always applies, because what is not alive is necessarily dead, the man who cannot see is obviously blind, and when it is not daytime it must be night time.

TULLIA: I understand now. What is the reason for this disparity?

VARCHI: The reason is that the contraries of exclusion do not have a mean in between, while the contraries of inclusion do. What is not black can be blue or some other color; what is not sweet can be sour, or have some other flavor.

TULLIA: I see that, but "beautiful" and "ugly" seem to belong to the class that admits of no mean between the two opposites.

VARCHI: It would seem so, but it is not so, for many things are found that are neither ugly nor beautiful.

TULLIA: Well, I could also find you some things that are neither alive nor dead, and others that are neither blind nor lit up by light.

VARCHI: Which ones?

TULLIA: Let me see, now: ah yes, these walls, those chairs.

VARCHI: Very ingeniously said but not correctly. An object may not be considered "dead" if it was never alive, or cannot be alive; neither can we call "blind" what is incapable of sight. How can we deprive something of a quality it does not possess, never did and never will possess? Poets are allowed to call rivers, forests, and other things "deaf," although these have no sense of hearing, because they are poets and must speak so [metaphorically]. But we must speak philosophically and therefore we should say that, among men as well as among women, there are some individuals who are neither beautiful nor ugly but who nonetheless by their own nature are made capable of receiving one or the other quality. Therefore, my rule does not apply here, contrary to what you say. So you see why good and wise men are more likely to be in love with people who are beautiful than with those who are ugly. Mind you, I do not wish to deny that beauty itself operates somehow in them too, to a great extent in fact; for beauty is a grace that allures, entices, and captivates those who get to know it. Rest assured that the more exquisite a person is, the more fervently he longs for beauty. As a matter of fact, in all parts of the universe, whatever they may be, wherever there is a greater measure of nobility and perfection, there is necessarily found a better and higher love as well. For this reason, as God is the highest goodness and wisdom, likewise He is the highest love and the highest everything.

TULLIA: I agree thus far and feel you have satisfied all my curiosity. The followers of Plato also turn their love toward those who are most beautiful, because they judge them to be the best and most intelligent individuals, although they are enticed by their beauty as well. In the same way you find that fathers or mothers both normally tend to show a preference toward the more good-looking among their children, though these are often the worst-behaved. Hence, we need not infer that there is any latent evil in the Platonic position. All I still have to find out is why they prefer to love those who are youthful, neglecting the aged. If people didn't know the real reason for this, they could harbor suspicions, which would not perhaps be totally unfounded.

VARCHI: They would be suspicious for a very good reason. If what they contend were true, I myself would be loud and clear. But you are mistaken. The reason why Platonic lovers seem to prefer youths is that the benevolence and affection, which we call "love" and see directed to young men, in time becomes friendship. Once its name is changed, it no longer seems to be the same feeling, but only then does love become truly perfect.[72] I know what I am talking

---

72. This too was a commonplace of love treatises. For example, in Giuseppe Betussi's *Raverta* we read: "Friendship is love that has grown old, and takes into consideration what is useful, good and pleasurable for one and the other partner" (*Trattati d'amore del Cinquecento*, p. 27). On this topic, Varchi wrote: "Nor should one believe that a good lover is rarer than a good friend. Even if it were

about, for when we cannot find pleasure in contemplating beautiful things, we can experience the enjoyment felt in admiring what is good, which is no less. We must remember that all creators, the more outstanding they are, the more delight they feel in their own creations. If natural parents derive great satisfaction from their children when these are good and virtuous, how much more must spiritual parents enjoy them! And as nothing is more useful than knowledge, so nothing is more rewarding than teaching, for those, of course, who do it for pleasure rather than for money.

TULLIA: Today I seem to be hearing things the like of which I never heard before. I feel sure, however, that you won't deny that many among those who love youthful partners, in the manner that you have been describing, cease to love them when the flower of their youthful beauty fades, and sometimes their love may even turn to repulsion.

VARCHI: I will not grant you this. If I did, I might as well have granted everything at the start of our discussion, because this is the whole gist of it. What other sign than this could be easier to recognize and more decisive in proving that their love is lascivious and as defective as the other people's?

TULLIA: How will you respond to my argument then?

VARCHI: I will deny it. What did you expect me to do?

TULLIA: Then you will be denying the truth, for the evidence points to the opposite of what you say.

VARCHI: You are wrong, I say!

TULLIA: Fiddlesticks! I'll have caught you out at the point where I least expected to.

VARCHI: I tell you it is not true. And I am surprised that you do not know that what cannot be, never was.

TULLIA: I am well aware of that, for the poet declares "How can it be, when it could never have been?"[73] So now you must respond to my point about what the evidence suggests.

VARCHI: Great matter indeed! The people that you had in mind could well feign a virtuous love but did not truly love. If they were philosophers, they did not love as philosophers should. When I say that this kind of love is far more complete and, consequently, far rarer than perhaps you think, you must believe me.

TULLIA: Unfortunately, I do believe it, and more wholeheartedly than you can imagine: perhaps even more than you do. Indeed, I do not deny that such love may exist. I admit it on your authority, for I know you would hardly

not so, good love always brings about good friendship, because when the use of the word lover comes to an end, that of friend begins" ("Sopra alcune quistioni d'amore," *Opere*, 2:559b).

73. Translation of "Com'esser può quel ch'esser non poteva," from Bembo's poem "Correte, fiumi, a le vostre alte fonti," *Rime*, 96.14.

assert it if you did not at least believe it to be true—I do not say "if it were true"—and also because I see no reason to dissuade me that it is so.

VARCHI: Many reasons would persuade us of this if the world were not so corrupted. You should know that, just as not all ages are fit to conceive and generate, so not all ages are equally disposed to learn. Often enough, either because the tendency is not in the nature of people, or because their desires and whims are subject to change—especially in the young—or because of a variety of contingent circumstances which are quite common in human affairs, loves are forsaken and friendships discontinued. This is due above all to greed, which reigns supreme almost everywhere in the world, or because of ambition, as we can see in *Alcibiades*.[74] But we are grappling with too complex a subject, while you have not yet discussed the third objection nor told me anything about the conversation you were engaged in when I arrived.

TULLIA: The originality and beguiling sweetness of your speech had made me forget the third objection. Even now, I'm not sure if my memory serves me well. But I think it was this: not all those who love with a vulgar type of love necessarily desist from their love when they have achieved their goal, because, in fact, many of them become even more ardently enamored after the physical conquest.

VARCHI: Yes, that is it.

TULLIA: There can be no doubt that when a thing is moving toward a particular goal and then reaches that goal, it ceases and no longer moves. This is because when the cause that gave rise to its movement, and which was the original goal, is lacking, then the effect, which was its movement, must also come to an end. Now, all those people who love in the vulgar way and desire merely to be carnally joined with the beloved object, as soon as they have consummated this intercourse, must desist from their movement and discontinue their love. Isn't that the case?

VARCHI: Very true. But let me ask: how is it that some lovers not only stop loving but turn their love into hatred? And others not only do not stop loving, but love more intensely?

TULLIA: Wouldn't you concede that no sooner has the physical act been achieved and intercourse consummated, then movement ceases and love must disappear?

VARCHI: Why don't you want me to grant what is true and cannot be denied, as far as this kind of love is concerned? Since this is desire and carnal ap-

74. In *Alcibiades* I, Socrates inquires of the rich Alcibiades, who is driven by ambition to enter the political arena, where he has acquired the wisdom to lead the Athenian people. We find that in Speroni's dialogue too ambition and practical considerations (*ambizione e utilità*) come in the way of love (*Trattatisti del Cinquecento*, 1:528).

petite, it necessarily follows that, once such appetite is quenched through copulation and physical union, love instantly disappears. But why is it that sometimes it changes into hatred and sometimes into greater love?

TULLIA: To give an answer to this last remark first, I say that you are contradicting yourself, because you do concede that love falls away in all beings when the carnal pleasure has been achieved, but then you ask me why sometimes it not only does not cease, but actually grows in intensity.

VARCHI: I do not know which of us is trying to aggravate the other. You take for granted what is still in dispute. I concede that love disappears in all those lovers, because it is so. Then I ask you why sometimes love grows—so that you may answer my question; for experience tells us that many lovers increase their love and, after reaching their goal, love more fervently than before.

TULLIA: I understood your argument, so I imagined that you had understood mine. What I'm stating is that once the carnal purpose has been attained, people are inevitably bound to lack the thrust and the stimulus that tormented and eroded their being up to a moment previously. This follows from the universal and self-evident proposition, which we have cited so often, that any thing that is moving toward a particular goal, once it reaches it, no longer moves. This is also because the senses of touch and taste, in the pleasure of which these lovers principally delight, are material rather than as spiritual as sight and hearing, and so they are satiated with immediate effect. Indeed, there are times when these senses surfeit the lovers so that they cause their love not just to stagnate but to mutate into hatred, apart from the causes that were mentioned a moment ago. In this way we have solved the first problem. As for the second issue, it is quite obvious that in the very moment when humans attain their desire, they automatically cease from their movement but do not discard their love; in fact, they often cause it to increase, because apart from their never being able to derive complete gratification from it, they retain the desire to enjoy the beloved object on their own, and by [continuing] union (hence this kind of love can never be completely lacking in jealousy). What is more, its acolytes become still more intemperate in their longing for carnal intercourse; they want to enjoy the thrill one more time, and still one more time after that, and so on. I'm not going to deny that this type of love may include a wide variety of possibilities: it may indeed allow for several different levels, according to the character and makeup both of the people in love and of those who are loved. For you may find that not only is one person more amorous than the other, but also that some are more prudent or of a more amiable disposition than others; so that this vulgar and lascivious strain of love can, at times and in some individuals, give rise to a chaste and virtuous love, just as a moral and virtuous love, because of some fault in either the lover or the beloved, may turn into one of the vulgar and lascivious variety. In the same way, many a plant may go from wild to domestic, or from domestic to wild, following its own pattern of growth and the nature of the terrain where it is found or transplanted. This, at any rate, is as much as I can think of saying to help the resolution of your doubts in the matter. I shall take what I say to be right only when I have your approval for it.

VARCHI: As for me, I am quite satisfied. There is nothing left for me to do but to thank you and, since it is getting late, ask you to keep the promise that you made me many times over. Had I not been certain of the kindness and courtesy of these gentlemen here, I might have feared being considered not just ignorant but presumptuous as well. So I beg them to excuse me for succumbing to your entreaties, while you must ask forgiveness for my behavior to yourself!

TULLIA: My dear Doctor Benucci, according to the agreement made, it is up to you to give a round of thanks to Varchi and to fulfil his request, for he has certainly deserved it.

BENUCCI: I am certainly not going to fall down on my obligations. Yet I must regret that I have insufficient time to carry out either one or the other of those two tasks, because all these hours of conversation seem not so much to have passed by us as to have flown on too speedy wings into oblivion. All of us together, Signor Varchi, and each on his own account, express a gratitude for your good nature that is perhaps hard for you to realize. This learned dissertation on the infinity of love was, by common consent, kept in reserve for you to deliver. We knew that you were supposed to turn up here on this occasion. I myself, and I am certain all these colleagues as well, feel the most intense possible satisfaction at having heard you. On my own and on their behalf, I thank you most warmly. We had also embarked on two other topics, and nobody was prepared to yield any ground on either of them. Each of us thought he had right entirely on his own side, and each was able to bring forth a plethora of justifications and learned quotations to support his case. Since we could find no other way of forging a consensus, we resolved to throw ourselves freely on your arbitration and to accept your deliberations and decision without any right of counterappeal. Nonetheless, a single condition was laid down, namely that in the dispute about the infinity of love nobody should raise a voice either to support or oppose the case except our Signora Tullia. The responsibility for the two remaining topics was assigned to me. But since the hour is now late and you, I am sure, must be feeling tired, if not put out, I will simply state the doubts without citing any of the arguments pro or con, or telling you who supported the one side rather than the other. You, with your usual unfailing kindness, will be so good as to comply with our lady hostess's wishes, and with our own, by declaring which side you hold to be right or wrong. Furthermore, if none of us finds it burdensome, we shall be able to fight it out at leisure some other time. Anyway, these were the doubts. First, there were some among us who held that all loves arise from private expediency and causation. In other words, whoever loves, loves principally from the standpoint of his own interest and personal advantage. Others among us rejected this line and held that there are people who love more for the sake of the other person than for their own benefit. The second issue turned on which is the more powerful type of love, the love that is imposed by destiny or the love which each of us chooses of his own will.[75]

VARCHI: I do not know what I should do first, to thank you for the great honor done to me, or to apologize for not being up to such a demanding task. When I came here, my dear Signor Lattanzio, I was far from expecting to be asked to debate so many questions, especially of this kind. I promise you that I will try my utmost on some other occasion and satisfy, if not your command, at least my debt.

BENUCCI: All we want from you is that you should tell us what your opinion is on the matter, without providing proofs or citing authorities. Please perform this favor for us in your own native city, since in Siena, or elsewhere, we would try to perform far greater ones for you, provided it was in our power to do so.

VARCHI: This is nothing compared to what I would do in your service and to satisfy you. As to the first point you raised, I believe that both parties are right.

BENUCCI: Take care, Signor Varchi, not to act like that mayor of Padua . . .

VARCHI: What I mean is that it is true and correct to say that all lovers derive their beginning, continuation, and ending from their own individual interests. For everything begins in itself and ends in itself, so all creatures firstly

75. Of the two doubts proposed here, the first one, on whether love is always motivated by self-interest, goes back to *Symposium*, 178–79. It became a favorite topos in the repertory of Renaissance *questioni d'amore*. In Leone Ebreo's *Dialoghi d'amore*, the question of whether one loves for the beloved's interest or for one's own is discussed on pp. 221–23. Here we also find the distinction between divine and human love, while the example of the arm and the head is on p. 57. The subject was taken up by Varchi in "Lezione terza, questione decima. Se qualcuno può amare più altri che se stesso," (*Opere*, 2:551–53). The second question—is love more powerful when chosen freely or when willed by destiny?—is similar to the *quistione* debated in Speroni's dialogue, where Grazia declares love to be a free human choice, while the Tullia character maintains the deterministic nature of love and believes it to be "heaven's violence on humankind" (*Trattatisti del Cinquecento*, 1:546, 555). Varchi briefly dealt with this second topic in "Sopra alcune quistioni d'amore. Lezione quarta" (*Opere*, 2:557a–558a).

and primarily love themselves and, consequently, do and say whatever they say and do for love of themselves. There is no doubt on this point, in my opinion.

BENUCCI: So was it wrong for one of us to argue that there were lovers who did not operate on their own account, but on behalf of the beloved?

VARCHI: I did not say that. If we talk about human love, that is to say from the moon down, it is correct to believe that each one of us loves what one loves primarily for one's own sake, because no one desires anything but what he does not have and would like to possess. But from the moon upward, among the heavenly intelligences, especially the Prime Mover, love is just the opposite of ours. God does not love in order to gain, for He has everything to perfection and in a manner that is unimaginable, let alone comprehensible to us. He loves and turns the heavens only thanks to His infinite goodness and perfection, which desires to bestow itself on all other things according to the nature of each, so that some receive more than others, in the same way as the sun: the light is shed equally on all things but is not received by all equally.

BENUCCI: That's precisely the way I took it. But what would your distinguished reply be about those individual lovers, who apart from exposing themselves to countless misfortunes and palpable dangers, may even choose of their own accord to die on behalf of the beloved object?

VARCHI: Just what you yourself would reply, Sir, that they choose it because it is the least of two evils.

BENUCCI: That is certainly true. Yet it seems as if they are showing more concern for others than for themselves.

VARCHI: It cannot be. They make their choice in view of what they consider the least damaging, if not the best, for themselves.

BENUCCI: And what greater damage can there be than death?

VARCHI: To live the way they would have to live. Anyway, don't you know that in perfect love—and this is what we are considering now—lover and beloved are one and the same, each one having changed into the other so that they are united?

BENUCCI: Yes, and that's why I can't see why one of them should willingly place himself more at risk than the other.

VARCHI: I know you are well aware that the beloved is the nobler of the two and that the lover, as the less worthy, must take all the risks in favor of the beloved. We can see that, likewise, the arm instinctively rises in front of the head, which is more important, and chooses to receive the blow in order to shield the head and save it.[76]

---

76. The example of the arm and the head can be found in Leone's *Discorsi*, p. 57.

BENUCCI: My view is that in the case of a perfect love relationship, when it is reciprocal, each partner is both lover and beloved interchangeably. Hence both of them, not just one of them more than the other, ought to be willing to run an equal amount of risk.

VARCHI: So they ought, and it happens quite frequently. Nonetheless, there is always a first lover, namely, the one who begins to love, and there is always a first beloved, the one of the two who is the first to be loved; although after their union has come about, each one is at the same time lover and beloved. And the gods—Plato tells us—reserve greater rewards for those beloved ones who let themselves die for their lovers than they do for the lovers who choose to go to their death for those beloved by them.[77]

BENUCCI: In this way it seems that lovers are nobler and more worthy than their beloved.

VARCHI: We already said that Plato grants it. Filone, on the other hand, holds an opposite opinion, and for a very good reason, as far as I can judge. The gods—Filone explains—reward more the beloved than the lover, for it is expected of the lover to behave and to suffer for the benefit of his beloved, and people generally believe this to be implied and required by the lover's debt.[78] But whatever the beloved does for the lover—and it is generally out of the graciousness and goodness of his character—deserves great praise from men and a greater reward from the gods. All of this, however, does not exempt him from returning his lover's love. But we do not have sufficient time to consider this point at present.

BENUCCI: I'm delighted that you have adduced the same reasons as those I brought up. However, with regard to that example you gave about the arm that does not hesitate to risk damage to itself in order to shield the head, I'm troubled by an inconsistency with what you said earlier, namely, that each object principally loves itself and performs every one of its functions for the expediency, enjoyment, and benefit of itself.

VARCHI: On the contrary, my example proves it quite clearly. Natural objects operate naturally, without realizing what they do and how they do it—just as fire is bound to ignite and water to moisten the objects in their paths, neither of them being aware of burning or of making things wet—for they are directed and monitored in their operations by God, just as the bolts that go toward their target are guided by the crossbowman and reach their goal without going astray. Hence the arm interposes itself between the blow

---

77. *Symposium* 180.

78. Leone offers for consideration a variety of opinions about the merits of lover and beloved (*Dialoghi*, pp. 228–233).

and the head for no other reason than to save the whole, for it knows that if the whole is destroyed the arm too is necessarily destroyed. For the very same reason and against their own nature, sometimes water rises and fire goes downwards. This occurs not simply because there is no void, but because if a void existed, the order of the universe and consequently the world would be destroyed and, without the world, there would be neither water nor fire. So it is true that all things in nature do what they do in order to keep and maintain themselves in life.

BENUCCI: With regard to the first doubt, I don't need to hear any more. What have you to say about the second one?

VARCHI: I must confess the truth to you. I do not understand it very well; and, besides, I see that we ought to consider the question of faith and predestination, which is a subject no less lengthy and difficult to handle than it is fraught with risks. In my judgment, we should put off this topic to an occasion when the most gracious and excellent Signor Porzio is with us, for only he possesses the depth and variety of knowledge necessary to satisfy your curiosity on this and on other such subjects with certainty and ease.[79] Had he dropped by today—as has been his custom of late—he would have saved me the effort of talking and would have arrived at a clear resolution of all your doubts without straining himself. But now it is time to take leave of Signora Tullia. We must not detain her any longer. Besides, I am still concerned that I might have disturbed your conversation, which cannot have been as serious and tiresome as you said, for I saw all of you amused and smiling.

BENUCCI: No, no: it is just as I told you. It is, however, true that we had started a dispute with our lady hostess. We wanted to prove to her something she knows much better than the rest of us, namely that she can be reputed as the most fortunate among all women. This is because there have been, and still are, few men in our society, whether they be excellent in military or literary pursuits, or in any other esteemed profession, who have not paid a tribute of affection and honor to her. I was drawing up a list of all of the gentlemen, the host of literary experts in all the various fields, the aristocrats, the princes, and the cardinals who have flocked to her house in different periods of her life— and still do—as to a universal and prestigious academy. What is more, all of these admirers have paid her respects and have honored her, and even now honor and heap their respects upon her. The cause of this lies in the very rare, not to say unique, endowments of her profoundly refined and conspicuously noble soul. I was already embarked on a seemingly endless enumeration of her admirers, and was still making important additions to it—almost against her

---

79. Simone Porzio, professor of philosophy at Siena and author of *De mente*, was a frequent visitor to Florence.

wishes—when she butted in on my speech and tried to cut me short. So then, at the precise moment when we heard your knock on the door and you turned up, I wanted to mention the city of Siena, where she is admired and venerated rather than merely treated with warm affection, especially by the most distinguished and virtuous of its citizens.

TULLIA: My dear Signor Lattanzio, if you do not quiet down, I shall break the rules of hospitality and lose my temper with you.

VARCHI: So far he hasn't said anything that I did not know already, and better than him, unless you believe me to be ignorant of what is common knowledge to all, and to ignore what all Italy, indeed the whole world, knows. So let him finish.

BENUCCI: I have no further points to make.

VARCHI: Please go on, for I want to know who are the Sienese who love her the most.

BENUCCI: I would have to give you a list of all the nobility in Siena, if you wanted to know the names of those who revere and love Tullia.

VARCHI: Tell me at least which ones are loved by her.

BENUCCI: I can't help you there, but I did think there were more of them than there actually are.

VARCHI: What do you know about it? My impression is that she refuses no one and gives a hearty reception to all.

BENUCCI: That is exactly what misled me. I know perfectly well that her generosity and courtesy are infinite and can be recognized by various tokens which I won't enlarge upon in her presence. But I was referring to those men for whom she cultivated some special and unusual affection.

VARCHI: You keep calling the cat a cat. What do you mean by that?

BENUCCI: I mean that perhaps a number of people are inclined to believe that Tullia is in love with them when in fact they are probably mistaken.

VARCHI: Why do you say this? I myself would hold her dearer if she were in love with somebody.

BENUCCI: So would I. But I take this line because earlier I mentioned by name, as one among all those who have loved and celebrated Tullia in prose and verse, Bernardo Tasso. I called him very fortunate, since he had been the object of such love on her part, and she told me I was wrong. I countered with the evidence and witness provided by Signor Sperone in his beautiful and learned *Dialogue on Love*, and she rebutted that, while she had loved Tasso, and did still love him, both for his qualities and in return for having been loved by him in such an unusual and overwhelming way, she had never felt jealousy for him.[80]

---

80. In Speroni's dialogue, the Tullia character, distraught at the news of Tasso's imminent departure, admits to being always jealous when in love and argues that there cannot be love without

VARCHI: Certainly, Signor Bernardo, as far as I have been acquainted with him, is a courteous and dignified figure and deserves all good rewards. Being in love with a person of such rare qualities as Signora Tullia, I consider myself lucky if she is not angry with me. Imagine then how happy it would make me to be in her good opinion and be cherished by her! I wonder what Signor Sperone was up to, for I know him to be a gentleman, as kind and considerate as he is learned and wise.

BENUCCI: It was thought to be so, for he displayed such affection for her! And who better than your good self can understand the power of jealousy?

VARCHI: Do you think me so jealous?

BENUCCI: I say so because in Padua you had a sharp lesson on this matter![81] But look, here is our Penelope.[82] It will be better to postpone the rest of this discussion for another occasion, so that these gentlemen in attendance can offer their contribution.

VARCHI: Yes, let us do that.

TULLIA: Yes indeed, but make sure all of you discuss topics other than my personal merits! Otherwise, I won't be able to listen and later thank you in an appropriate and decorous fashion, as I should like to. However, wherever my poor supply of knowledge and discrimination may have proved lacking, the courtesy and the extensive learning that are shared by the present company should come to my rescue.

---

jealousy. Grazia, on the other hand, maintains that perfect love does not allow for jealousy (*Trattatisti,* 1:513–15). This too was a popular *questione,* going back to Lysias' and Socrates' views in Plato's *Phaedrus* (231–234c; 237b–239c).

81. In Padua, Varchi had been beaten by Piero Strozzi's men. There were allegations of Varchi's having appropriated some books of Strozzi, as well as of his having seduced Piero's young brother, Giulio, with whose education he had been entrusted (Pirotti, *Varchi,* p. 15). The envy of slanderous opponents is a frequent subject in Varchi's writings. See "Sopra l'invidia. Lezione una" (1545); "Ragionamento nel quale si favella della invidia o dell'odio" (1545); "Sopra un sonetto del Bembo. Lezione una" (*Opere,* 2:582–611, 568–82). Cf. footnote 8. Lecturing on Bembo's sonnet, Varchi presented the standard view that rational love can be without jealousy, while carnal passion cannot.

82. Penelope was Tullia's sister.

INDEX